MAKING YOUR OWN

PATCHWORK

and Quilting

ISABEL DIBDEN WRIGHT

NH
NEW
HOLLAND

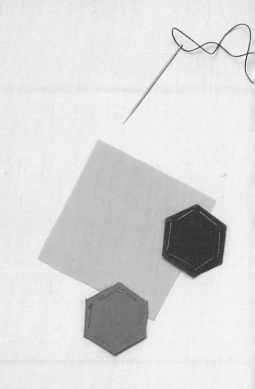

This book is dedicated to my father and also to my mother, who did not live to see its publication.

First published in the UK in 1994 by
New Holland (Publishers) Ltd
37 Connaught Street, London W2 2AZ

The author would like to thank the following embroidery students at The Manchester Metropolitan University for the use of their work in the book:

p. 10 design by Jayne Huckvale; p. 20 top left: Donna Rumble; pp 20–21 top, Jayne Huckvale; bottom, Elizabeth Brimelow; p. 29, top: Esther Cox; p. 63 Amanda Sharp; p. 76 Margaret Wilson.

ISBN 1 85368 224 1 (hbk)
ISBN 1 85368 327 2 (pbk)

Creative editor Pauline Butler
Assistant editor Sue Thraves
Art director Jane Forster
Photographer Shona Wood
Illustrator Terry Evans
Calligrapher David Harris

Typeset by Ace Filmsetting Ltd, Frome, Somerset
Reproduction by Scantrans Pte Ltd, Singapore
Printed and bound in Singapore by Kyodo Printing
Co (Pte) Ltd

Contents

Introduction

There is a long and fascinating tradition of patchwork and quilting throughout the world, and early examples of the crafts have been found in places as far apart as China, Siberia, India and Egypt.

The earliest patchworks were made from animal skins and later, from fabrics sewn together to create larger pieces for bedding and clothing. In this way precious scraps of fabric could be saved and recycled. Initially these scraps were probably joined in a random, somewhat crude fashion, but once the fabrics were cut into shaped patches, patterns began to emerge. The stitching used to hold the layers together was probably initially very simple, but the makers began to create patterns from the stitching (which also strengthened the fabrics considerably), and the myriad quilting patterns began to develop. The

basic principles of patchwork and quilting remain just the same today.

My interest in patchwork and quilting developed when taking a degree in embroidery during the nineteen seventies. A revival of interest in the subject was taking place at the time, and quilts were beginning to be shown in art galleries, where they could be viewed as 'art' objects.

Since then I have continued to be inspired by the subject because of the wealth of creative possibilities to be found in both patchwork and quiltmaking.

There is great enjoyment to be received from both crafts, and from the end results of the gentle, repetitive actions. Patchwork and quilting are very calming activities.

To be able to make an object that can be both beautiful and useful from such simple materials is very special.

Chapter 1
Getting started

Before you begin

If you are new to the subject of patchwork and quilting do not be tempted to launch straight into a major project! Many people make this mistake and end up dissatisfied, with unfinished projects hidden in the backs of cupboards. It is a pity that so much wasted effort goes into these false starts. Time is well spent learning skills and developing an understanding of the subject first. Only then should an ambitious project be undertaken.

Always start with something small and simple, and gradually build up to a large piece of work. A quilt is a major undertaking that could take weeks or months to complete, and may also be a fairly large financial outlay. So, it is only sensible to plan a piece like this carefully, and not to rush into it with undue haste.

Before beginning a piece of work consider some of the following questions:
1 Who is the piece being made for?
2 What is the piece being made for?
3 Do I have the skills that are needed?
4 How much time do I have for this work?
5 Is there a deadline (birthday or other occasion) that needs to be met?
6 Can this piece be made in the time that is likely to be available?

7 Can this piece be made within a budget that I may have?

Time spent reflecting upon these questions will really be time well spent.

You will need to equip yourself with some basic tools, and with some fabrics and threads described in this chapter.

Once you have collected some equipment you will then be ready to learn some skills, and to begin to make your own items. A diverse range of patchwork and quilting methods are described in later chapters.

Tools and equipment

You will need some basic tools for patchwork and quilting:
Scissors
Needles
Dressmaker's pins
A thimble
A tape measure
Beeswax
A dressmaker's marker pen and pencils
Drawing pencils
An iron
You will be able to do almost everything mentioned in this book with these few simple tools. However, there are some other pieces of equipment that you may need,

such as a quilting frame and a sewing machine. The kind you choose will depend upon the amount and type of sewing you intend to do.

Always buy the very best tools and equipment that you can afford, and look after them. It is true to say that if these are used with care and respect, they will repay you with years of good service.

Store your tools and equipment in a container that is suited to the way you prefer to work. For example, if you carry your work around with you, a box or small work basket will make your tools portable, but if you tend to use a particular room to work in you will need to organize your equipment differently.

There are many (expensive) gadgets currently on the market especially for patchwork and quilting, but consider carefully before purchasing any of these, as many are destined to lie unused.

Scissors: Good scissors are vital. Make sure that fabric scissors are only used for fabric, as anything else will spoil them immediately. You will need large cutting out shears and small, sharp-pointed embroidery scissors.

Make sure that the scissors are comfortable to use. If you are left-handed do try to purchase left-handed scissors for this reason. If you carry your scissors around with you, carry them in a sheath or case for safety, and to protect the blades.

You will probably also need scissors for cutting paper, to use when making pattern templates. However, a craft knife is more accurate for cutting strong paper and card.

Needles and needlecases: Equip yourself with a good range of quality needles, and never use needles that are dull, blunt or rusty: throw them away!

A selection of betweens, sharps, crewel and tapestry needles will be suitable for most sewing. Needles should be carefully stored in a dry place. A good way to keep a variety of needles together is to make a needle book, with pages of wool flannel. The lanolin in the flannel will prevent the needles from rusting, and each page can be devoted to a different type of needle.

Pins and pincushions: Buy good quality, fine steel dressmaker's pins, and make sure you have plenty. Glass-headed pins are the easiest to see in a piece of work, as well as when they fall on the floor! Wedding dress or lace pins are excellent for use on very finely woven fabrics.

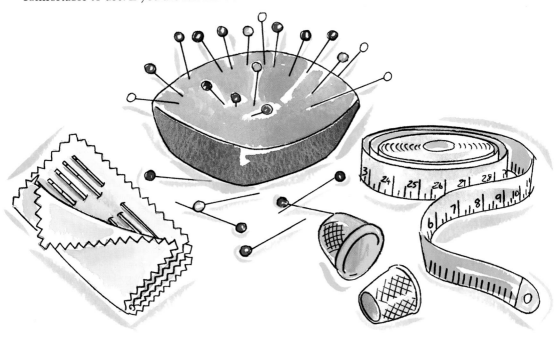

For the most delicate fabrics do not use pins: use fine needles as pins instead.

Have one pincushion to carry around, and if you use a sewing machine, attach another pincushion to this.

Never allow your pins and needles to become muddled up together, especially in a box, as you will waste much time when you are searching for either.

Thimbles: Persevere if you are unused to using a thimble; you will need to use one if you are going to do any hand quilting. There are a number of types of thimble, made from a variety of materials. If you do not like the end of your finger to be enclosed, you may prefer to use a tailor's thimble, which is open at the end, allowing ventilation. Make sure the thimble you use fits you well.

A tape measure: An obvious piece of equipment, but if purchasing one, make sure it is durable, with clear markings.

Beeswax: This is available in small cakes or in containers, and is used to strengthen thread. This is done by running it across the beeswax. Beeswax also prevents thread tangling and twisting, and is particularly useful for hand quilting.

Marking pencils: You will need some form of marker for marking cutting lines and quilting/sewing lines. There are numerous types available, but coloured water-soluble pencils are recommended. White shows up well on dark colours, and pale blue or similar is good on white or other pale colours. Take care when using some of the pens that are water or air soluble, as they can create a very thick, inaccurate line. Also, the lines may not vanish as readily as the manufacturers claim.

Quilting frames: The traditional way of hand quilting a large piece was to use a quilting frame. Quilting frames can be purchased from specialist suppliers, or simple frames can be constructed easily from four lengths of wood with webbing attached to the two long sides. The sides can be held in place with G clamps. This type of frame can be taken apart for storage or transportation. If you make your own frame you can make it in a size to suit yourself, and to suit the available work space.

Quilting rings: These are like large size embroidery rings. They can be used for medium and large size pieces of work, but they can be a little awkward to use when

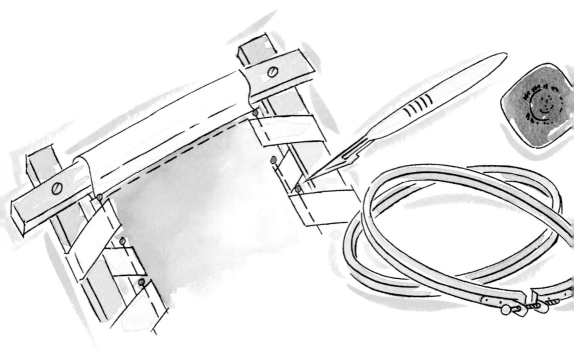

quilting a large quilt. Their advantage is that they take up far less space than a frame.

Rectangular quilting frames: These are available in different sizes, and are suitable for small or medium size pieces of work. Many quilters consider these frames to be an improvement on ring frames.

A sewing machine: This is undoubtedly the major piece of equipment you are likely to purchase. Before you commit yourself, look at the models available, and ask for advice. A good tip is to find out what type of machine your local school or college is using, as they will probably have quality sewing machines that are simple to use and durable. As with all equipment, aim to buy the best quality you can afford.

Look for a model that is simple to use and to thread up, and that is not too heavy. This is important if you need to transport the machine from place to place.

You will need a machine that does straight stitch and zigzag (satin stitch), it should also be able to sew in reverse. Make sure that you can change the feet on the machine easily. You will need the following feet: straight stitch, zipper foot, darning (embroidery) foot and a walking foot. The walking foot is especially useful for machine quilting, and for sewing bulky fabrics and pile fabrics such as velvet, which tend to creep or move whilst being sewn.

A rotary cutter and cutting mat: Rotary cutters are useful if you are cutting out large quantities of fabric, as they do speed up the job. A cutting mat (available from graphic suppliers, art shops and needlecraft shops) needs to be used with the cutter. The cutting mat is also invaluable when cutting paper and card with a craft knife.

Drawing equipment: Some basic tools will be needed for marking templates and for drawing out designs. Try to buy this equipment from an art shop or graphic suppliers, as they should have a good choice of quality drawing aids.

You will need: pencils, a metal rule at least 30 cm (12 in) long, a craft knife or scalpel, an eraser and a set square. A protractor and a pair of compasses would be very useful if you intend making your own templates. Artists' and designers' materials such as coloured pencils, water-based paints, squared paper, coloured paper and sketchbooks would all be needed if you intend working on your own designs.

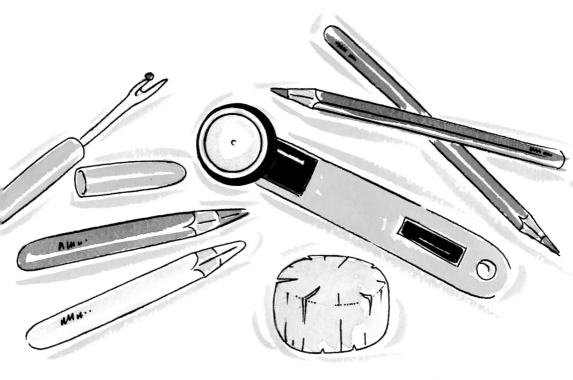

Fabrics

You will need to make a collection of fabrics before you start making patchwork or quilts. Begin looking for interesting fabrics, and collect information on suppliers and stockists for future use.

Keep all the fabrics you collect away from sunlight, damp, dust and insects. A cupboard with shelves where the fabrics can be stored away from daylight is ideal. Never store fabrics in plastic bags, and always keep them folded and grouped in some way; either by colour, or fabric type. Regularly check through your fabric collection, and pass on fabrics that you know you are not going to use. Someone else may be able to use them.

Remember that you do not need to buy all the fabrics you may wish to use. You can recycle all sorts of fabrics from clothes and household textiles.

You will probably be able to purchase threads as you need them, so you will not need to amass a large collection initially.

The choice of fabric is fundamental to the success of any piece of patchwork or quilting. Be adventurous with your choice of fabrics. Many people have preconceived ideas about what types of fabric are suitable for patchwork, frequently believing that they must use small floral prints. This is not the case, as the examples in this book show.

If your knowledge of fabrics is limited, it is worth spending time finding out about them before undertaking a major project. Visit good fabric shops and look carefully at what is in stock. Handle the fabrics, your sense of touch will begin to inform you about the tactile qualities of the different fabrics; this will become more sensitive the more you use it. The appearance of the fabric is obviously of primary importance, but do not underestimate the importance of its tactile qualities. It is a natural reaction to want to touch a piece of cloth.

Collecting fabrics: Regularly look in fabric shops (remember fabrics change from season to season), and look in charity (thrift) shops and remnant bins for oddments. If you see a fabric that is of interest buy a small amount, you will soon build up an interesting and inspiring collection. Remember also, to look for fabrics when you travel anywhere, especially if you go abroad.

A good collection of fabrics is necessary when planning patchwork and quilting. Keep a look out for fabrics in interesting colours and textures, as these will inspire and influence your designs.

Natural fibres

Natural fabrics are the best for patchwork and quilting. These are either derived from animal sources: silk, wool and other animal fibres, or from plants: cotton, linen and other plant fibres.

Silk: Since it was discovered over 4,000 years ago, silk has been highly valued for its luxurious qualities. It is both delicate and hardwearing, and soft, with good draping qualities. It is also surprisingly strong, elastic and resilient and, because silk absorbs moisture, and does not conduct heat, it is comfortable close to the skin in all kinds of temperatures.

Silk is a fine filament, extruded by silkworms and spun to form a protective cocoon. This filament consists of two threads coated with a viscous gum which hardens in contact with air, thereby binding the threads together. It can be dyed and printed in many beautiful colours, but because of its absorbency, colours are likely to run when the silk is washed. Therefore, most silks require dry-cleaning.

Examples of silk fabrics include: bourette, brocade, chiffon, crêpe de chine, doupion, georgette, habotai, organza, pongee, satin, shantung, taffeta, tulle, tussah, velvet.

Wool: Wool cloth has been spun and woven for over 12,000 years, ever since sheep were domesticated. Wool produces a versatile fabric which has the ability to be cool in the heat and warm in the cold, and it absorbs moisture without feeling wet. Every wool fibre has a natural elasticity that allows it to be stretched by as much as one third and then spring back into place. Its complex cellular structure also enables it to absorb moisture vapour but repel liquid – just try to soak up water with a wool cloth. There are three main categories of wool; merino, crossbred and carpet. Merino sheep produce the finer qualities of wool.

Wool can be dyed to produce colours that are strong, deep, rich or bright. However, the durability of the colour can be affected by sunlight and repeated washing. Wool has an important safety factor too, as it is difficult to ignite, and any flame produced spreads slowly and is easily extinguished.

No synthetic fibres have yet been developed to successfully combine all these desirable characteristics.

Fabrics such as cotton, linen, silk and wool are all natural fibres. All have special characteristics which make them attractive in their own right. They are best for patchwork and quilting.

Examples of woollen fabrics include: blanket, botany, challis, delaine, felt, flannel, tweed, jersey, plaid, plush, serge and Viyella (50% wool and 50% cotton).

Cotton: Cotton has been used in making textiles for at least 5,000 years, and evidence exists that the cotton plant grew in India and Mexico over 7,000 years ago. It was known to the ancient Indians, the pre-Inca civilisation, the ancient Egyptians, the Greeks and the Romans.

Cotton is a soft fluffy vegetable fibre which grows from the seed pod of the cotton flower. It is cultivated in humid, sub-tropical conditions, and the best quality cotton is produced where the growing season is fairly wet and the picking season warm and dry.

Cotton is the most widely used of all the textile fibres. It is durable, has good absorbency, is hygienic because it withstands high laundering temperatures, and is low cost. Creasing can be overcome with ironing, or with the use of modern crease-resistant finishes, or by blending with synthetic fibres.

The mercerization of cotton is a common finish for both yarns and fabrics. This process (which involves treating the cotton with caustic soda) causes the fibres to swell. The benefits of this are increased strength and absorbency, and added lustre due to light reflection from the smoother surface.

Examples of cotton fabrics include: buckram, bump cloth, calico, canvas, chambray, cheesecloth, chintz, corduroy, drill, denim, flannelette, gingham, lawn, mull, muslin, organdie, piqué, poplin, sateen, scrim, seersucker, towelling, ticking, velveteen and voile.

Linen: Linen is the oldest textile material in the world. Fragments have been found dating back to 8000 BC. Linen is produced from the fibrous stem of the flax plant, which grows well in a temperate, moist climate, and in good soil.

The stems of the flax are gathered and retted (soaked in tanks of water, or left to lie in dewy fields), to loosen the fibre which is separated from the rest of the stem. It is then dried and scutched (this is a process that removes the coarse, woody and other

Woven checks and stripes are invaluable additions to any patchwork makers' collection, as are cotton fabrics with small-scale prints.

foreign matter from the other fibres). Lengthy labour-intensive production methods make linen expensive.

The longer the linen fibre, the finer the resultant fabric, and the higher its cost. Short, coarse fibres are used for upholstery and coarser fabrics; longer fibres are used for sheeting, handkerchiefs and dress fabrics.

Of all the textile fibres linen washes best. When linen is washed a minute micro-molecular layer is removed from around each fibre. With each wash the surface comes up new without affecting its strength or durability. It is the strongest natural fibre, and increases in strength when wet.

Linen is highly absorbent, and gives up its moisture into the surrounding atmosphere more rapidly than any other textile. That is why it is so comfortable to wear in warm or humid climates.

Linen fibre is often blended with other fibres such as cotton (generally for economy) or polyester (to make it easier to care for). Linen union is a very hard wearing furnishing fabric with a linen weft and a cotton warp.

Examples of linen fabrics include: crash, handkerchief linen, Holland linen, scrim, and union.

Fillings and interlining

There are various types of filling, known as wadding (batting), for quilting. These are made from man-made and natural fibres, and all produce different effects. It is worthwhile spending time trying them out to see which produces the effect desired for the piece being made.

Polyester: This is inexpensive and readily available in different weights: light weight, medium weight and heavy weight, which is only suitable for tied quilting. It is available in white and a charcoal colour (suitable for dark fabrics). It launders well and is quite easy to use.

Cotton: Cotton wadding is used extensively in the Far East for quilts and quilted garments. It produces a less bouncy effect than polyester, but can be more difficult to quilt. This type of wadding sometimes has a papery skin on one side, and can be used folded double (the way it is sold), or unfolded to produce a lighter effect.

Colour is a very important consideration when making patchwork and quilts. Aim to build a collection of fabrics in a wide colour range.

The sample on these pages show just some of the many different methods of patchwork and quilting. The designs draw on a variety of sources for their inspiration, including traditional pieced work, log cabin and shadow quilting. Some of the designs are quilted by hand, others by machine. The fabrics chosen include plain and printed cottons, silks, sheers, felt and yarns.

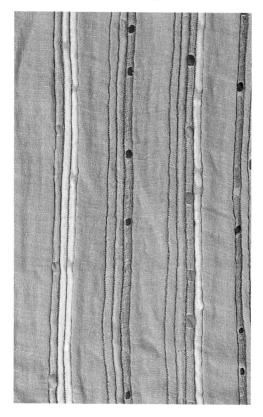

Cotton/polyester: A good combination is a lightweight wadding composed of 80% cotton 20% polyester, blended and bonded together to prevent fibre migration. This combines the best qualities of both fibres. (Cotton/polyester mix is also sometimes known as 'cotton classic' or loomtex keyback batting.)

Wool: Carded sheep's wool was traditionally used as a filling for quilts. The wool was laid directly on the backing cloth and covered with the top fabric. It is much easier to use wool in the form of a woven fabric (an old wool blanket, for example), or as domette (also known as icewool). This warm, lightweight knitted interlining can be used singly or in layers. It is not available necessarily everywhere.

Silk: There is nothing to compare with the softness, lightness and warmth of a garment or quilt with a silk filling. This is obviously best used with other silk fabrics. This filling is expensive and only available from specialist suppliers in some countries.

As you develop your patchwork and quilting skills you will find that different types of thread are best suited to particular applications. As with fabrics, collect threads for future use.

Threads

You will need threads for sewing, tacking (basting) and for quilting. The use of natural fibres are recommended as much as possible. They handle better than synthetic threads, and generally, the colours and textures are much more interesting. In short, there is no comparison between the colour, handle and durability of a woollen thread and an acrylic one.

Sewing threads: Always use a reputable brand, these will probably be more expensive, but will have a better range of colours and will be stronger and easier to sew with. Always use a sewing thread, not a machine embroidery thread, or tacking (basting) thread.

Buy large size reels of white, ecru, grey and black threads; you will probably find that you use more of these colours and they are always useful to have in stock.

Mercerized cotton thread has a smooth, silky texture. As well as creating this characteristic appearance, the mercerization process slightly increases the strength of the thread, so that a finer thread can be used.

Another type of thread that is widely available is a spun polyester thread which is fine and quite strong. Care needs to be taken

when pressing anything sewn with this type of thread, as a hot iron will melt the thread.

If using a fabric made from a natural fibre it is appropriate to sew this with a thread that is also made from a natural fibre.

Silk thread is available in small reels, and is expensive, but it is beautiful to hand-stitch with, and the colours are superb.

Tacking (basting) thread: This is a soft fluffy thread available on large reels. The fluff ensures that the thread grips the fabric, while its softness means that it can be easily removed without damaging the fabric. Never use coloured tacking thread on light coloured fabrics, as a dye can stain. Also, avoid using tacking thread for permanent sewing as it is not strong enough.

Quilting thread: This thread is sold by quilting suppliers. It is slightly thicker than ordinary sewing thread, but it is only available in a limited range of colours.

Threads for quilting: Look around for different types of thread for quilting. There are some interesting embroidery threads and weaving, knitting and crochet yarns that are excellent for hand quilting, and also for different forms of machine quilting.

Embroidery threads: These are suitable for different types of hand quilting. Silk threads are excellent for quilting fine silk fabrics. Coton à brôder, soft embroidery cotton and cotton perlé are good for creating a bolder line (similar to the effect achieved by kantha quilting from Bangladesh).

Linen threads are strong and lustrous, with slight variations of thickness.

Woollen crewel and tapestry threads and knitting yarns are ideal for tufting and tying, and for Italian and shadow quilting. Stranded cotton is also suitable for tufting and tying.

Machine embroidery threads: This is finer than sewing thread, and is not as strong, but can be used for machine quilting and for machine appliqué. It is often mercerized and is available in a wide range of colours. There are some interesting fancy threads for machine embroidery that are made from wool, rayon, and metallic thread. Good embroidery equipment stockists will stock these or obtain them for you.

Aim to choose threads made from natural fibres for patchwork and quilting. The colour range is subtle, and finishes range from matt to lustrous. Glossy, metallic threads also have their uses.

Colour

Colour is probably the most important element in patchwork, and is also of primary importance in quilting. The first thing that attracts us to a piece of patchwork is the colour, above pattern, technique and the surface qualities.

Some people are fortunate enough to have an intuitive colour sense and are naturally able to put colours together in a pleasing or exciting way. Others need to develop this skill, and this can be done by experimenting with the use of colour. It is all too easy to hold a closed attitude to colour, and to 'play safe', always choosing the same, familiar colours that we know we are able to combine fairly successfully.

Before beginning a quilt you will need to plan your colour scheme. The choice of colour may be partly governed by the use that the piece will be put to, or by the room the quilt will be used in.

Get ideas by arranging fabric scraps together, or 'play' with colour chips cut from household paint charts. The subtle colour variations here can be a useful design aid.

Always try to choose your colours in daylight and, if your quilt is designed for a particular location, try the colours in that place, in different lights, as you may find that they look quite different.

Colour balance: Remember that a colour cannot be considered in isolation, colours always appear quite different when put next to different colours. The proportion of colour also has an effect; even proportions can be very different in appearance to a large amount of one colour and a small amount of another colour.

Tone is of equal importance to colour. Tone is the amount of lightness or darkness that the colour contains; white being the lightest and black being the darkest.

Distribution of colour also has an effect, as small amounts of broken colour look quite different from large blocks of colour.

Colour schemes

Different colour schemes that you may consider are as follows:

Monochrome: Here one colour is used from light tints to dark tones, or a combination of black and white can be used. Proportion is of importance in this type of scheme.

Colour plays a very important part in every piece of patchwork. For example, to appreciate how the impact and balance of the design would change, imagine any one of these samples worked in the colours used for an adjacent piece. When planning a design, decide on the effect you would like to achieve, and then try placing fabrics close to one another until you are satisfied.

Simple bands of colour take on different effects depending on their arrangement. When planning your designs, experiment with fabrics, to see how the same colours can appear hot or cool, dramatic or serene.

Harmonious: Generally composed of colours that are found beside each other on the colour wheel or in the spectrum, as for example, green, turquoise, blue. The effect achieved is generally quite soft with no strong contrasts.

Complementary: Two colours that complement each other, or bring out the qualities of each other. These are opposites on the colour wheel, as for example, red and green. One of the colours can be dominant, the other used to provide an accent or keynote in the design. Relatively small amounts of a second colour can dramatically change our perception of the other colour.

Neutrals: Subtle effects can be produced with the use of neutral colour fabrics and threads, in their undyed, natural state. They can vary from delicate beiges and ecrus to the rich browns of some of the linens and wild silks.

Discordant: As discordant notes can be used in music, so discordant colours can be used together to produce unusual effects. Pink and yellow used together are an example.

Atmospheric: The colours chosen may express an atmosphere, mood or emotion. For example, certain colours can be joyful, some tranquil and others melancholic.

If you experiment with colour and enjoy using it, your colour sense will soon develop.

Design
This is the area that many are least prepared to tackle, holding the incorrect idea that it is particularly difficult. It is worth remembering that so many quiltmakers in the past created beautifully designed quilts with no artistic training whatsoever.

Many are prepared to develop their technical skills to a very high standard, yet feel unwilling or unable to develop their creative or inventive skills. Because of the fairly formal nature of patchwork and quilting this is a relatively easy area in

which to design or plan a piece of work.

Tremendous satisfaction is to be gained from designing and making up your own designs, however simple they may be. (See page 12 on the different stages required when planning a piece of work – this could be referred to as a design.)

You may like to collect design ideas, and find that inspiration can come from anything that you see. Very simple ideas can be made into eye-catching quilts; often the best designs are the simplest. Look at traditional quilts to see what can be achieved with patchwork made from a single shaped patch – there are a great many possibilities.

Simple designs can be made by drawing ideas out on to squared paper or graph paper. A little practice will soon produce a number of ideas that will probably refine and develop fairly quickly.

Adapt designs if you do not feel competent to make up your own designs, as through this experience you may find that you are able to create your own designs.

It is best to approach designing (or any other type of work) from a point of stillness. Allow the mind to become quiet, you may be surprised at the ideas that then present themselves. Note down any ideas that you may have, as you may not recall them all unless you do. Carry a small notebook or paper pad in your pocket or bag to make a sketch, or make a note of anything you see that may be useful in the future. It is well known that some of the best ideas were first

The fan design, above, shows how a symmetrical design can be varied by repositioning the blocks. In this symmetrical quilting design, opposite top, a large area of richly coloured stitching is balanced by the smaller yellow stitching.

jotted down on envelopes! The idea can always be drawn out more carefully later, but if it is not noted down immediately it will soon evaporate and fade.

There is no right way of designing, one person's approach can be totally contrary to the way another person works.

Patchwork and quilting can be defined as arranging shapes within a given space. There are different ways of arranging these shapes, and some of them are as follows:

Symmetrical: Here shapes are arranged so that the two halves of the design are the same. These designs are balanced and can be very ordered.

Asymmetrical: Here the two halves of the design can be quite different, there needs to be a balance between the elements in the two halves.

Central medallion: This has been a popular patchwork and quilting design for about two hundred years. Begin with a central block or image, then add borders around this. These borders can become wider in proportion to their increasing length. (*See the* **Black, white and red quilt** page 45 for an example of this type of design.)

This black and white central medallion design is based on a log cabin block.

In log cabin patchwork all the strips are worked round a central square.

Blocks: Another design form that has always been particularly popular. Here individual blocks that can vary in size are arranged to create a repeating pattern. The blocks are generally square and are all the same size. This is a good design to begin with, as a number of blocks can be made, and these can be moved around in different arrangements. Try making a number of blocks and then spend time playing with the way they can be positioned. Make a note of the different pattern variations that can be formed, or photograph them. You can then select the arrangement that is more pleasing. (*See the* **Fan quilt** page 39 for an example of this type of design.)

Stripes: Strip quilts are easy to design, and are composed of vertical stripes that run from the top to the bottom of the quilt. These stripes can be contained within a border, which can be the same width as the stripes. Quilting patterns can be arranged in the same way.

When designing it is important to consider what you want to achieve in a design. Some useful aspects to remember are scale, balance, harmony, contrast, composition, distribution, simplicity, complexity and rhythm. Which of these do you want to achieve in the quilts you are designing or making? Designing is an activity to enjoy and spend time over, just as much as the activity of making and stitching.

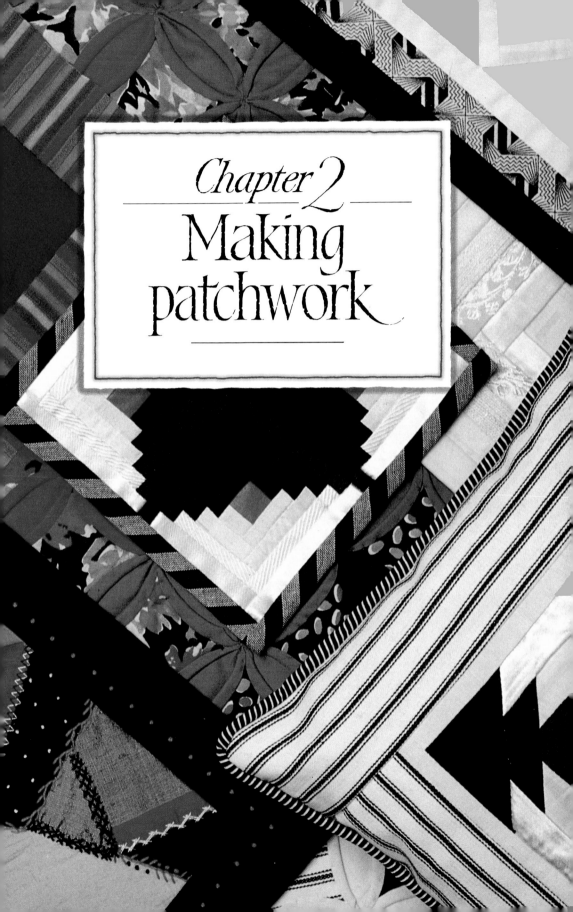

Chapter 2
Making patchwork

Patchwork is about pattern and colour, whereas quilting is essentially concerned with creating surface qualities. A range of patchwork methods are described in this chapter, from ones that are simple and quite easy to master, to others that require precision and skilful execution.

Crazy patchwork

This method makes use of random shaped patches of fabric. These are applied to a backing cloth, such as calico (muslin), and lines of embroidery are stitched over the joins between the patches.

Crazy patchwork was particularly popular in the second half of the nineteenth century, when it was most frequently made from brightly coloured silks, velvets, ribbons and other trimmings, and was heavily embroidered with complex stitch patterns.

Traditional crazy patchwork uses hand-stitched embroidery to embellish the random patches.

REQUIREMENTS
Backing fabric (for hand method)
Fusible interfacing (for machine method)
Fabric scraps in a variety of colours and textures
Tacking (basting) thread (for hand method)
Embroidery threads (suitable for hand or machine method)
Sewing threads (machine method)
A sheet of white paper (machine method)
An iron
Basic sewing tools

Making hand-stitched crazy patchwork:
This is the traditional method of applying the patches. The decorative embroidery can be worked by hand or machine.

Preparing the fabrics:
Cut a piece of fabric for the backing, allowing at least 1 cm (⅜ in) seam allowance around the edge, and pin and tack (baste) the first patch to one of the corners.

Adding the patches:

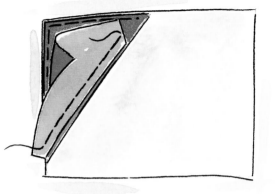

Take a second patch and turn a narrow hem on the edge which will overlap the first patch. Place over the raw edge of the first patch, pin and tack (baste) along turned edge.

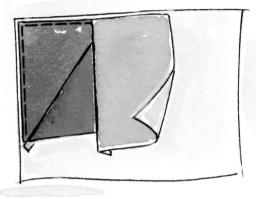

Apply a third patch over one of the raw edges of either the first or second patches, and pin and tack (baste) this in place.

Continue to apply patches in the same way until the whole of the backing fabric is covered. It is necessary to keep observing the overall look of the piece, to keep a balance between the colours, textures and scale of the patches, as it is very easy for the size of the patches to get progressively smaller without you noticing.

Embroidering the patches:

Stitch the patches to the backing cloth using a small hem stitch along the joins between the patches. Remove the tacking (basting) threads as you stitch.

Embroider along the joins between the patches. A variety of stitches: feather, herringbone, chain stitch are traditionally associated with this form of patchwork.

Making machine-stitched crazy patchwork:

A quick way of making crazy patchwork is to back the patches with a heat fusible interfacing. The fabrics can then be bonded to the backing fabric with an iron, before securing them with plain or decorative machine stitching.

Preparing the fabrics:

Cut out a piece of iron-on fusible interfacing to the required size. Place this with the fusible side up, on to the ironing surface. Arrange the fabric patches over the interfacing, butting the edges together as much as possible. (Only very small amounts of the interfacing should be left exposed.)

Securing the patches:

Once the fabric patches are in position on the backing fabric, place a sheet of clean paper over the work and press with a hot iron. Remove the paper immediately to prevent it bonding to the interfacing.

Machine stitching the patches:

Stitch over the entire fabric using a straight stitch or zigzag stitch. It is not necessary to sew round each patch. For interest, work the stitches with different coloured threads.

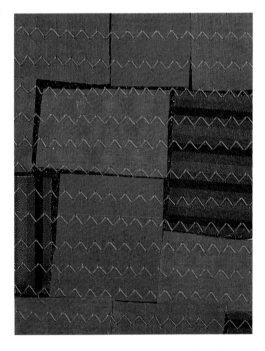

Machine-stitched crazy patchwork offers the opportunity to make use of zigzag stitching.

Crazy patchwork cushion

Crazy patchwork can be very effective when worked in a monochrome colour scheme. This cushion is made from fabrics in shades of white, cream and ecru, and has a hand stitched patchwork centre. The shapes are embellished with embroidery stitches.

Finished size 42 x 42 cm (17 x 17 in) square.

REQUIREMENTS
*(All measurements are for fabric 140 cm
    (54 in) wide, and are approximate.)*
*32 x 32 cm (12½ x 12½ in) square of cotton
    backing fabric*
*A variety of fabric pieces in shades of
    cream, white and ecru*
30 cm (⅓ yd) cream silk
25 cm (¼ yd) striped silk
2 m (2¼ yd) medium piping cord
50 cm (½ yd) cream cotton
*Embroidery threads to complement the
    colours of the chosen fabrics*
Basic sewing equipment
A sewing machine
An iron
*(See **How to make and finish a quilt** page 85
    for details on making piping.)*

1 Following the method for hand-stitched crazy patchwork, work the centre of the cushion front, by assembling the pieces on to the backing fabric.

2 Seam two strips of cream silk 3 x 32 cm (1¼ x 12½ in) on to two opposite edges of the patchwork. Press them back. Seam two strips 3 x 34 cm (1¼ x 13½ in) on to the other two edges. Press these back.

3 Seam two pieces of striped silk 7 x 34 cm (2¾ x 13½ in) to two opposite edges of the cream border, and seam two pieces 7 x 45 cm (2¾ x 17¾ in) to the remaining two edges.

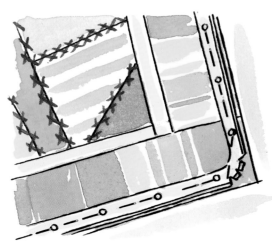

4 Make 180 cm (72 in) of piping from the cream silk, and tack (baste) this in position around the edge of the cushion front.
5 Cut two pieces of cream cotton for the cushion backing 30 x 45 cm (12 x 17¾ in). Turn-in and make a narrow hem along one of the long edges of both pieces of fabric.
6 Place these pieces over the cushion front with the right sides of the fabric facing, and with the hemmed edges overlapping in the centre. Stitch close to the edge of the piping. Turn out to the right side.

The striped border and piped edge create a striking frame for the crazy patchwork panel on this cushion. The design, in cream and soft earth tones, is perfect for a simple wooden chair.

Patchwork with paper templates

This type of patchwork is particularly suitable for small scale, intricate designs that demand precision in execution. It is quite time consuming and calls for dexterity, yet surprisingly it is frequently the first form of patchwork that people attempt. All too often unplanned quilts made from large hexagons are embarked upon, but few are finished!

With this in mind, it is best to undertake a small project as a first attempt at using paper templates. A cot quilt, a cushion or even a pin cushion are realistic pieces.

All sorts of geometric shapes can be used for this form of patchwork. The most popular are: squares, triangles, diamonds, rectangles, pentagons and hexagons, and any combinations of these.

REQUIREMENTS
Paper and card
A craft knife and cutting mat
A sharp, hard pencil or fine pen
A ruler, and metal rule
A marker pen or pencil
Sharp scissors
Fabrics
Tacking (basting) and sewing threads
Basic sewing tools

Geometric shapes such as hexagons, triangles and squares are favourite shapes for small scale patchworks made with paper templates.

Cutting paper templates:

Always cut paper templates exactly the size that the finished patch is to be. These templates must be cut very accurately, as any small errors will create problems when the patches are sewn together. Use a sharp pencil to mark out the cutting line on the paper, and cut out the paper templates with a sharp craft knife or scalpel and metal rule. Make the templates from old letters, magazines and computer paper. It is also possible to re-use the templates once they have been removed from a piece of work, so do not throw them away.

Cutting the fabrics:

Cut fabric patches with a seam allowance that is about 1 cm (⅜ in) larger than the paper templates. The size of the seam allowance will vary depending upon the type of fabric being used. Fabrics that fray easily will need a larger seam allowance than those that are more stable. Mark the cutting line on the reverse of the fabric using a suitable fabric marker.

Fitting the paper templates:

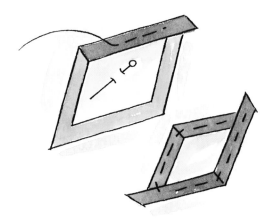

Place the paper template centrally on the wrong side of the fabric patch, and fold the seam allowance over on to the paper. Tack (baste) the fabric patch to the paper template, folding in the seam allowance carefully and stitching through corner folds.

stitch. Use a matching thread if possible, or use a mid tone grey for the whole piece, as this will not be too obtrusive. The stitches should not pass through the papers. If the stitches are too large it will be possible to feel the needle going through both fabrics and papers.

Removing the templates:
Continue to join patches together. The tacking (basting) stitches can then be taken out. In a large piece of work the papers can be removed as the work is progressing, it is only necessary to leave the papers in place at the edge of the work, where they are needed to keep the patches in shape.

(Do not be tempted to trim any fabric away, as any points that seem to be sticking out will be underneath the piece when the patches are sewn together. If they are trimmed back, the points may fray.) The tacking (basting) stitches can be up to 1 cm (³⁄₈ in) long. Use a thread which contrasts with the fabric colour, and preferably in a lighter shade, as bright or darker colours can leave stains when the thread is removed.

Joining patches:

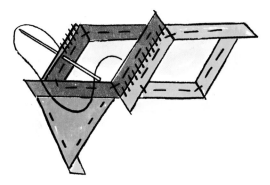

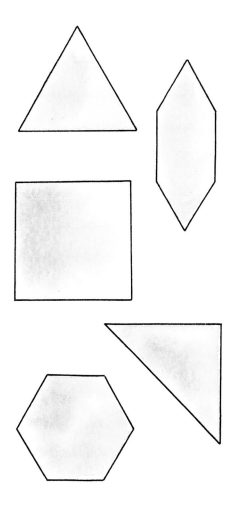

Press the patches once they are tacked (basted) to the papers. To sew the patches together, place them together with right sides facing, and work a small oversewing

Make a collection of template shapes from card and paper, or buy them in plastic or metal.

A fan design quilt

This single quilt is made from plain and striped silk and cotton fabrics using a combination of bright and dark colours. The strong colours chosen for the hand-stitched fans contrast with the dark blue cotton used for the background. The quilt is constructed in blocks; each one is machine quilted, then joined by machine and finally hand tied.
Finished size 180 x 120 cm (78 x 48 in).

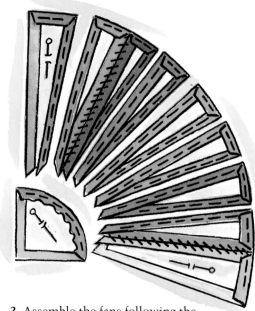

REQUIREMENTS

(All measurements are for fabric 140 cm (54 in) wide, and are approximate)
2.80 m (3¼ yd) dark blue cotton
Small amounts of a wide variety of plain and striped silk in: bright yellow, burnt orange, rust, cerise, red, purple, lilac
2.80 m (3¼ yd) lightweight polyester (loomtex keyback batting) or cotton classic wadding
2.80 m (3¼ yd) fine white cotton (muslin, mull or similar)
7 m (7¾ yd) cotton backing fabric to match the colours of the fabrics for the fans
Tacking (basting) thread
Matching sewing threads
A white marker pencil
6.20 m (6⅞ yd) piping cord
One skein blue cotton perlé embroidery thread
Card and paper for templates
Basic sewing equipment
A sewing machine and zipper foot
An iron
*(See **How to quilt** page 78 for details on tied quilting, and **Making patchwork** page 36 for details on making patchwork with paper templates, and **How to make and finish a quilt** page 85 for details on making and attaching piping.)*

Making the patchwork:
1 Cut fifteen 32 x 32 cm (12⅝ x 12⅝ in) squares of dark blue cotton.
2 Cut out card and paper templates for the fans. Using the card templates, mark and cut out the silk fabrics. (Take a generous seam allowance if the fabrics fray easily.)

Note: If you prefer, you can re-arrange the fan blocks to create a different effect. The fans could be arranged to form half circles, or a fan block could be placed in each corner of the quilt.

3 Assemble the fans following the directions for patchwork using paper templates. Do not turn back the edges of the two outside patches and the bottom edges of all the patches, as shown. Sew the tapering shapes together, then apply the quarter

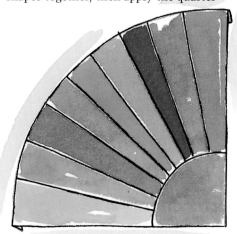

circle patch over the inner raw edges. Sew this in place with an invisible slip stitch. Press the completed fans gently.
4 Carefully remove the tacking (basting) stitches and the paper templates. (These can be re-used for another project.)

This colourful fan design is made with the paper template method. Each design block is completed and then arranged in this striking way.

Trace fan templates here and transfer them on to card and paper. Make up and machine quilt fifteen blocks following marked quilting lines. Copy plan to join blocks in formation shown.

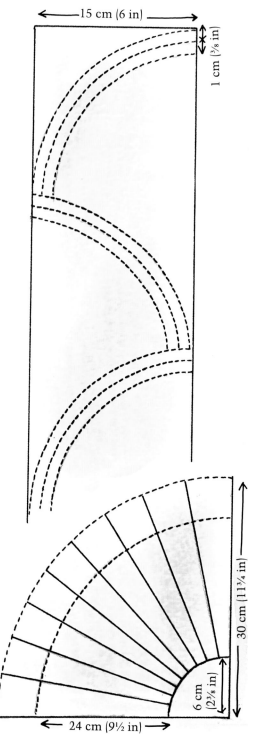

5 Position the fans on corners of the blue cotton squares. Pin and sew along the outer edges of the fans using an invisible slip stitch. Press the squares. Trim away excess blue cotton fabric from beneath fans, to leave seam allowance of at least 1.5 cm (⅝ in).

Assembling the squares:
1 Cut fifteen 32 x 32 cm (12⅝ x 12⅝ in) squares of wadding and white cotton.

2 Assemble the squares with a layer of white cotton, a layer of wadding, and the patchwork fan. Tack (baste) round the edge of the squares.
3 Machine quilt each of the squares using matching threads, as quilting design.
4 Join the squares together, with right sides of fabric facing, taking 1 cm (⅜ in) seams, in the arrangement shown in quilt plan. Press all the seam allowances open.

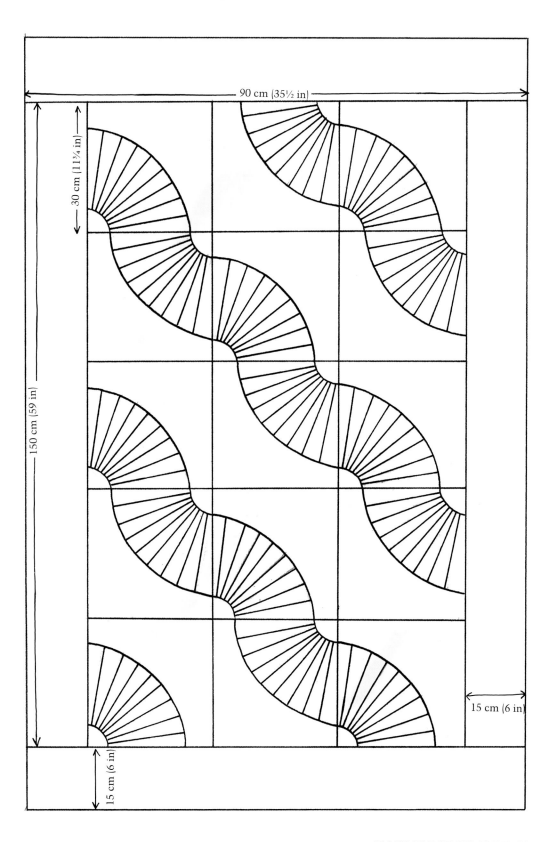

90 cm (35½ in)

30 cm (11¼ in)

150 cm (59 in)

15 cm (6 in)

15 cm (6 in)

Making the borders:

1 Cut two 122 x 17 cm (48 x 6¾ in) strips each of dark blue cotton, wadding and white cotton, and two 182 x 17cm (79 x 6¾ in) strips each of the same.
2 Use the white marker pencil to mark out the quilting pattern on the four blue strips.
3 Tack (baste) the layers of blue cotton, wadding and white cotton together. Machine quilt the four strips following the marked pattern.
4 Pin, tack (baste) and machine-stitch the two long strips to the two long edges of the centre of the quilt, with right sides of fabric facing, and taking 1 cm (⅝ in) seams. Press all the seam allowances open. Sew the other two strips in place on the other two sides.

Piping and finishing the quilt:

1 Cut bias-cut strips of the silk fabrics to cover the piping cord. Machine-stitch the strips together taking 1 cm (⅜ in) seams. Press all the seam allowances open. Continue joining the strips to the same length as the piping cord.

The piped edge adds a neat finishing touch to this tied quilt. The colour of the backing fabric is also an important part of the design.

2 Pin and tack (baste) the fabric strip round the piping cord. Pin and tack (baste) the covered piping around the edge of the quilt, with raw edges level. Machine-stitch the piping in place using a zipper foot. Press the piping towards the edge, and the seam allowance towards the centre of the quilt.
3 Cut the backing fabric about 183 x 122 cm (79 x 48 in). Place the quilt with right side facing downwards, and position the backing fabric, with right side up, on top. Turn in the seam allowance, pin and invisibly slip stitch the backing close to the edge of the piping.
4 Tie the layers together using the dark blue perlé thread, making the ties at regular intervals all over the quilt.

Piecing

In this form of patchwork, pieces of fabric are seamed together by hand or machine without the aid of templates. The individual patches are joined into strips or blocks, and these blocks are joined to form larger units until the design is complete.

This method is quick and easy to work on a machine, and tacking (basting) can be kept to a minimum. Simple patched blocks may not need tacking (basting); they can be pinned and stitched, and the pins removed as you work.

Piecing is particularly suitable for large projects like bed-sized quilts and throws, as although the resulting shapes may not be as precise as those worked with paper templates, the time factor makes the method an attractive option.

REQUIREMENTS
Fabrics and templates
A marker pen or pencil
A ruler and straight edge
Dressmaking pins
Matching sewing threads
A sewing machine
An iron

Preparing the patches:

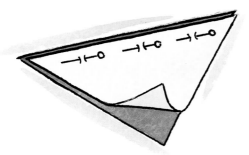

Draw round the template shapes on to the wrong side of the fabric, taking note of provision for seam allowances. Some instructions on bought templates require you to add a seam allowance round the template outline before cutting out, while others include the seam allowance and require you to mark the seam line inside the template outline after cutting out. After cutting out and marking the seams, pin two patches together with right sides facing, using the pins to check that the lines match.

Sewing the patches:

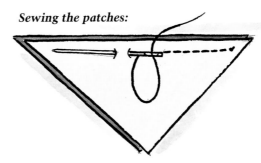

Stitch along the seam line by hand or machine. If by hand, use a small running stitch and stitch from one edge of the fabric to the other. If by machine, use a medium size stitch and sew across from one edge of the fabric to the other.

Pressing the seams:

When joining dark and light coloured patches together, press the seam so that the allowance is pressed towards the darker patch. This will prevent the dark colour showing through on the right side.

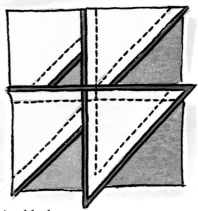

Making blocks:

Continue to join and press the finished patches as described, then join them into larger strips or blocks. Press all the seams in the same direction.

Piecing curved seams:

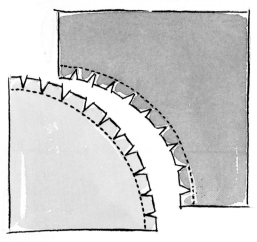

These require accuracy, but with a little practice smoothly curving seams can be achieved. It is important to carefully clip both curved edges at regular intervals before stitching. Make these clips reach almost to

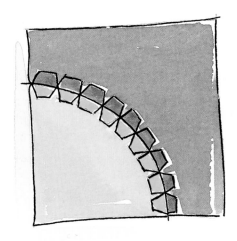

the seam lines. After clipping, carefully pin the fabrics together taking care to match the sewing lines.

Pieced black, white and red quilt

This dramatic quilt could be used on a double bed, or as a wallhanging. The colour scheme was derived from the light and dark arrangement of fabrics usually associated with log cabin patchwork. The single red square in the centre relates to the red square often found in the centre of each block in log cabin designs, and is said to represent the hearth in the centre of the cabin.

As all the other measurements relate directly to the size of the centre patch, the scale of the piece could be changed quite easily by changing the size of this. The design is easy to construct, and starts with the centre patch.

Finished size 183 x 183 cm (72¾ x 72¾ in) square. Seams of 1 cm (⁴⁄₁₀ in) are included in all the given measurements.

REQUIREMENTS
(All measurements are for fabric 140 cm (54 in) wide, and are approximate.)
10 cm (⅛ yd) red cotton
2 m (2¼ yd) cream cotton or spun silk
3 m (3¼ yd) black cotton
1 m (1⅛ yd) black and white striped cotton
3.70 m x 50 g (4 yd x 2 oz) polyester wadding (batting)
3.70 m (4 yd) backing fabric
Basic patchwork tools and equipment
A quilting hoop or frame
*(See **How to quilt** page 62 for details on wadded quilting and page 64 for details on using a frame.)*

Making the patchwork:
1 Make pattern templates for the triangles from stiff paper or thin card to the sizes listed on the cutting diagram, and mark them with their colour and sizes. Cut out a 9.5 x 9.5 cm (3⁷⁄₁₀ x 3⁷⁄₁₀ in) square from red cotton. Mark a seamline on the reverse of the fabric, 1 cm (⁴⁄₁₀ in) in from the edge.
2 Cut out the cream and black triangles. You will have a total of sixteen triangles of each colour, and four of each size. Mark the 1 cm (⁴⁄₁₀ in) seam lines on the reverse of each triangle.

This elegant pieced patchwork quilt owes much of its impact to the bold use of colour, as the design itself is very simple; on a smaller scale it could be a single block. The use of a contrast patterned fabric for the backing gives the design an unexpected twist by adding a change of scale.

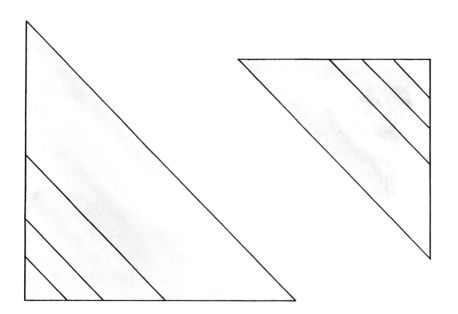

3 Stitch the smallest four black triangles on to the red square, following the instructions given for piecing, and using the quilt pattern as a guide.

4 Again, referring to the quilt pattern, stitch the smallest four cream triangles on to the black triangles. Continue by sewing on alternating groups of black and cream triangles until all the triangles are joined.

Making the borders:

1 Cut out two strips from black fabric 124 cm (49 in) long x 4.5 cm (1⁸⁄₁₀ in) wide. Stitch these on to the two opposite sides of the cream triangles. Cut two more strips 134 cm (53 in) long x 4.5 cm (1⁸⁄₁₀ in) wide, and stitch these to the other two sides. (It will probably be necessary to join fabric strips to this length.)

2 From striped fabric cut out two strips 134 cm (53 in) long x 4.5 cm (1⁸⁄₁₀ in) wide, and two strips 144 cm (57 in) long x 4.5 cm (1⁸⁄₁₀ in) wide. From cream fabric cut two strips 154 cm (61 in) long x 4.5 cm (1⁸⁄₁₀ in) wide, and two strips 164 cm (64½ in) long x 4.5 cm (1⁸⁄₁₀ in) wide. Following the quilt pattern and starting with the striped strips, stitch these in place along the edge of the black strips, joining them on opposite sides as before.

3 Cut two 20.5 cm (8¹⁄₁₀ in) wide strips from black fabric, sufficiently long enough to match the length of the cream border. Stitch these on to two opposite sides of the quilt, then cut two more strips long enough to make a square when sewn in place. Sew these to the other two sides.

4 From cream fabric, make another border from strips measuring 4.5 cm (1⁸⁄₁₀ in) wide, and add these on opposite sides as previously described.

5 From striped fabric cut four 7 cm (2⁸⁄₁₀ in) wide strips for the binding. Stitch these in place as for the other borders.

Assembling the quilt:

1 Cut the wadding (batting) and the backing fabric. Join the widths as necessary to the same size as the finished patchwork. Press the seams open on the backing fabric.

2 Assemble the quilt as follows; lay the backing fabric flat with wrong side facing upwards. Lay the wadding (batting) over this, then the patchwork, right side facing upwards, on top. Pin and tack (baste) the layers together.

Quilting and finishing the patchwork:

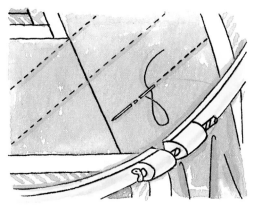

1 Fit the prepared fabrics into the quilting frame and, using cream thread, quilt the layers with diagonal lines of stitching spaced 10 cm (4 in) apart.

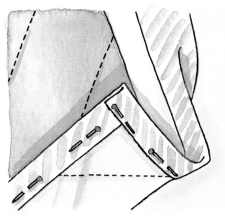

2 Fold the binding fabric over to the back of the quilt, and turn in the raw edges to make a bound edge 2.5 cm (1 in) wide on both sides of the quilt. Pin and invisibly stitch the binding. Finally, use an iron to gently press the edge of the quilt.

Suffolk puffs

These are as their name suggests, puffs of fabric, each one created by drawing up the edges of a fabric circle. A number of different fabrics are suitable for Suffolk puffs, and striped fabrics are particularly effective, as are fine silks, cottons and transparent fabrics such as voile, net and filmy chiffon.

Suffolk puffs can be made in different sizes, but avoid using thick fabrics such as velvet and corduroy for small puffs, because the bulk of the fabric prevents the puff from being drawn up sufficiently.

REQUIREMENTS
Fabrics
Circle template
A marker pen or pencil
Sewing thread
Washable toy filling (optional)
Small, pointed scissors
Basic sewing tools

Preparing the fabric circles:

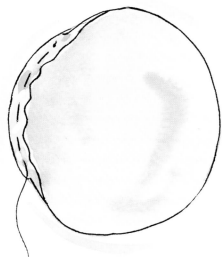

Cut the circles of fabric about twice the size that you intend the finished puff to be. Using a strong thread that matches the fabric, begin with a knot on the thread and a back stitch (this thread is going to be drawn up, and needs to be securely attached). Run a gathering thread around the edge of the puff, turning a narrow hem (about 5 mm (⅕ in) deep) as you sew. The stitches do not need to be tiny, two stitches to 1 cm (⅜ in) is sufficient.

This delightful form of patchwork can look particularly effective on a small scale, as these colourful miniature puffs show.

Gathering the puffs:

Draw up the thread tightly, secure with a knot, and take the thread through the centre of the puff, and cut it off. The end of the thread is then lost inside the puff. Flatten the puff by gently pulling it into shape.

Joining the puffs:

Place two puffs together with right sides facing, and make some small oversewing stitches along the edge of the two puffs, where they touch. Suffolk puffs can be joined in rows or in a circular arrangement.

Padding the puffs:

Puffs can also be padded. To do this, insert a small amount of washable filling before the gathering thread is drawn up. Push a small piece of fabric into the hole after the thread has been secured to prevent the padding from showing. Do this using the points of some small, sharp scissors.

Cathedral window patchwork

This hand-stitched patchwork gives the illusion of being quilted, but the effect is created by squares of fabric that are folded and stitched together. Cathedral window does make use of fairly large amounts of fabric, so allow for this when planning a design. The most suitable fabrics to use are fine cottons such as lawn, or fine poplins.

Fine silks, transparent cotton voile or organdie are also suitable, and can be used to create interesting effects, but these fabrics are more difficult to handle.

REQUIREMENTS
Plain and patterned fabrics
A base patch template 15 x 15 cm (6 x 6 in)
   square
A window patch template 4 x 4 cm (1½ x
   1½ in) square
A marker pen or pencil
Basic sewing tools
An iron

Folding the base patch:

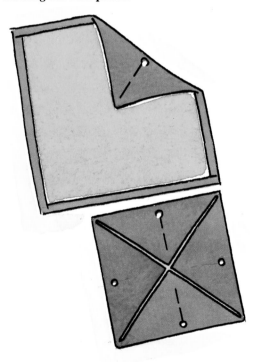

Use the template to cut 15 x 15 cm (6 x 6 in) squares of plain fabric, and press a narrow hem of 6 mm (¼ in) all round the edges. Fold each corner of the square into the centre, and pin into position.

Pinning to shape:

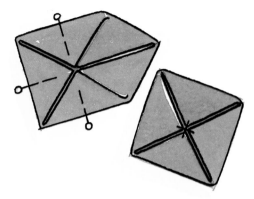

Fold each corner of the square into the centre and press in position, removing the first set of pins when the new pins are inserted. The square should now measure 7 cm (2¾ in).

Stitching the base patch:

Use small stitches through to the back of the square to secure these four points. Make a second square following the previous directions. Join these two squares together by placing them together with right (folded) sides facing, and oversew along the edge.

Adding the window patch:

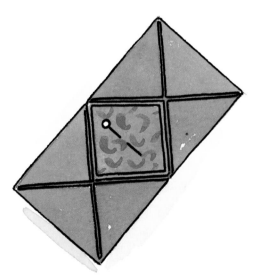

Use the template to cut a piece of fabric 4 cm (1½ in) square. (This may be the same as the fabric used for the base patch, or use a contrasting fabric.) Place this over the join between the two squares and pin in place.

This example of cathedral window patchwork shows how a printed fabric can be combined with a plain one to create a delicately textured effect. To copy the idea, choose two fabrics which are exactly the same shade of white.

The versatility of cathedral window patchwork is shown in this design, which is made up of black and white ticking, narrow, black-and-white-striped cotton and plain, cream and black fabrics. The effect is striking in its graphic simplicity.

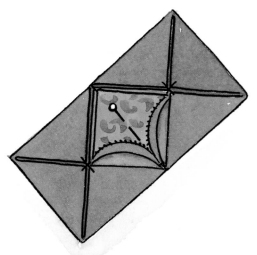

Stitching the window:

Turn the edges of the fold over the raw edge of the window piece, and sew them in position, using a stab stitch through to the back of the square. You will find that the fabric edges roll naturally to make the curved shape associated with this patchwork.

Make further pairs of squares and join them on to the first two squares. Continue in this way to complete a design.

Cathedral window wall piece

Display this design as a wall hanging, or back it with a matching plain fabric and make it into a large cushion. You could also surround it with borders made from the same fabrics as in the design.

Finished size of the piece is 62 x 62 cm (24 x 24 in) square.

REQUIREMENTS
*(All measurements are for fabric 140 cm
    (54 in) wide, and are approximate)
1.50 m (1¾ yd) black cotton lawn
50 cm (⅝ yd) red cotton lawn
25 cm (⅜ yd) blue cotton lawn
25 cm (⅜ yd) pattern (a) cotton lawn
50 cm (⅝ yd) pattern (b) cotton lawn
Matching sewing threads
Basic patchwork tools and equipment
An iron
(See **How to make and finish a quilt** page 86
    for details on hanging methods.)*

This example shows how subtle variations of pattern and colour can effect the design. In some areas the curved, folded edges of the patches create a contrast with the floral inserts, while in other areas they create larger splashes of colour.

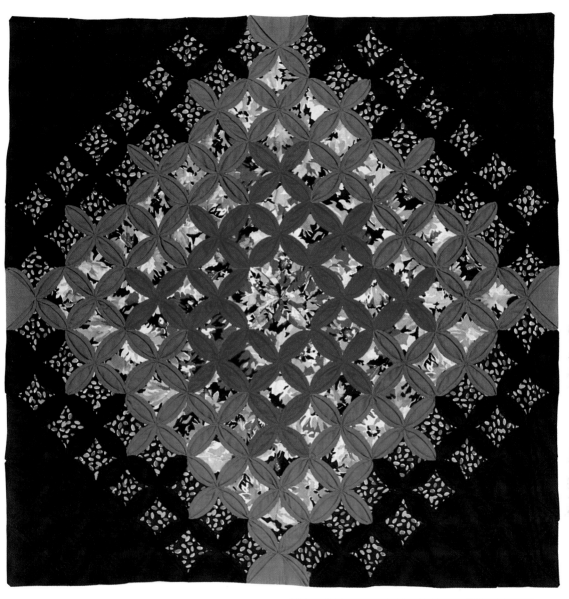

This design epitomizes cathedral window patchwork. The bold 'leading' ranges from brilliant red, through grey to black, framing the jewel-bright colours glimpsed in each small 'window pane'.

1 Following the directions for making cathedral window patchwork, sew the squares together in the arrangement shown.
2 If the piece is to be used as a wall hanging, following the instructions for this, or make up the patchwork into a cushion. If adding borders, cut all the fabrics and join them in the desired sequence.

Note: *It is worth making a collection of photographs of real stained glass windows, to give you inspiration. Brilliant plain silks and cottons, and small scale 'splashy' prints are invaluable for creating the illusion of stained glass panes.*

Another way of approaching the patchwork method would be to try to create a view beyond the window. By carefully positioning plain and patterned fabrics behind a 'leaded' frame, you could suggest a landscape.

Variations:
Achieve different effects by changing the positions of the squares. Follow the diagram to produce this variation.

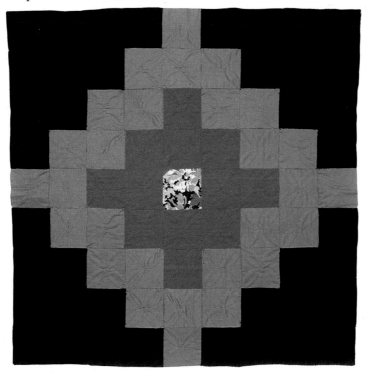

From the back, cathedral window patchwork simply looks like a series of small squares, neatly joined with small, oversewn stitches.

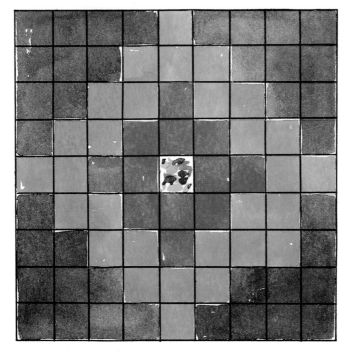

Note: When assembling a piece of cathedral patchwork, you may find it more comfortable, because it is less bulky, to sew only a few background squares at a time before adding the insert patches. Make up rows of completed windows and then stitch these together.

Log cabin patchwork

In this form of patchwork strips of fabric are applied around a central patch to create a block. Groups of blocks can be joined together in various ways, to create striking patterns that frequently give the illusion of being three-dimensional.

Fabrics for log cabin:

Fabric scraps can be used, since the patchwork strips used are often fairly small. Also a variety of different types of fabric may be used in the same piece; it is good to contrast dull with lustrous, or textured with smooth fabrics in this form of patchwork.

Classic log cabin patchwork can be worked as here, with fabrics in 'modern' prints. Each patchwork block has a central red square surrounded by dark and light strips.

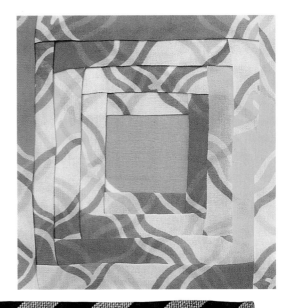

Working log cabin:
Log cabin can be worked by hand or machine (in fact it can be more durable and more precise if worked by machine). Log cabin worked by hand looks a little softer, and of course, hand work is very portable. (If sewing by hand use a small running stitch, if by machine use a medium length straight stitch).

Careful planning of colour, fabric and design are vital to achieve good results with log cabin. It is also important to be organized, preparing the backing fabrics and cutting strips before beginning to sew.

REQUIREMENTS
Fabric and fabric scraps .
Calico (muslin) for backing
Fine marker pen or a sharp pencil
Ruler
Tacking (basting) and sewing threads
Basic sewing tools

Designing the blocks:
First decide upon the size of the individual blocks that you intend to make, the width that the strips will be, and the size of the central square. This will usually depend upon the finished size of the piece.

Making a 18 x 18 cm (7 x 7 in) block:

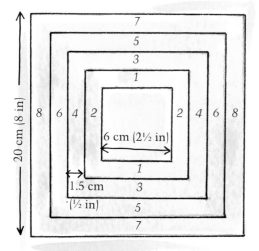

Cut a piece of calico (muslin) 20 x 20 cm (7¾ x 7¾ in) square. On one side follow the log cabin diagram to carefully mark the sewing lines with a fine dressmakers' marker pen or with a sharp pencil.

> **Note:** *You can check that you have positioned the log cabin strips correctly by holding the fabric to the light, with the wrong side of the work towards you. You will be able to see the strips through the fabric to check their position.*

Adding the central patch:
Cut a piece of fabric 8 x 8 cm (3¼ x 3¼ in) square for the central patch. Pin and tack (baste) this to the right side of the calico (muslin), which is the side that does not have the markings on.

Adding the first four strips:

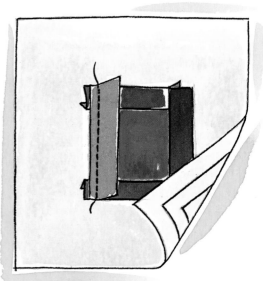

Cut the first two strips of fabric 8 x 3.5 cm (3¼ x 1½ in). Pin these on opposite sides of the central patch, in line with the two edges of the patch. Turn the fabric over so that the markings can be seen, and stitch along the two lines where the strips have been pinned on the other side of the calico (muslin). Press the strips back.

Cut two more fabric strips 11 x 3.5 cm (4¼ x 1½ in) and sew these to the other two sides of the central patch, following the instructions for the previous strips. Press the strips after stitching.

The second round:

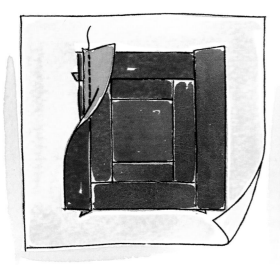

Cut two strips 11 x 3.5 cm (4¼ x 1½ in) and stitch these on to the first two strips that were applied (strips 1 and 2). Press.

Cut two strips 14 x 3.5 cm (5½ x 1½ in) and stitch these to strips 3 and 4. Press.

The third round:

Cut two strips 14 x 3.5 cm (5½ x 1½ in) and stitch these to strips 5 and 6. Press.

Cut two strips 17 x 3.5 cm (6¾ x 1½ in) and stitch these to strips 7 and 8. Press.

The fourth round:

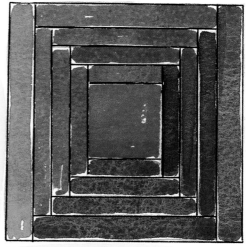

Cut two strips 17 x 3.5 cm (6¾ x 1½ in) and stitch these to strips 9 and 10. Press.

Cut two strips 20 x 3.5 cm (8 x 1½ in) and stitch these on to strips 11 and 12. A block is now completed. Press strips back.

Joining blocks:

Further blocks are joined by placing them together with right sides facing, and by sewing along the outer line on the wrong side of the fabric.

Pineapple log cabin cushion

Because of the small scale of this piece it would be a good introduction to this form of patchwork. It is a variation of log cabin patchwork and is also sometimes known as 'windmill blades' because it can create a sense of movement.

You could if you wish, make a group of blocks, and join them to make a larger piece.

Finished size 23 x 23 cm (9 x 9 in) square.

REQUIREMENTS
(All measurements are for fabrics 140 cm (54 in) wide, and are approximate.)
15 x 15 cm (6 x 6 in) square calico (muslin)
4 x 4 cm (1¼ x 1¼ in) square red cotton
20 cm (¼ yd) black, cream and white cottons or silks
25 cm (¼ yd) black and white cotton ticking
25 cm (¼ yd) black and white striped cotton fabric
1 m (1¼ yd) medium piping cord
15 cm (1¼ yd) black and white spotted fabric for cushion back
Matching sewing thread
A marker pen or pencil
A ruler
Basic patchwork tools and equipment
A sewing machine
An iron
A cushion pad 22 x 22 cm (9 x 9 in) square
*(See **How to make and finish a quilt** page 85 for details on making piping.)*

1 Mark out the sewing lines on the calico (muslin) backing square, using a fine marker and following the pattern. Pin and tack the red fabric square on to the unmarked side of the calico.
2 Pin four 3.5 x 2 cm (1⅜ x ¾ in) cream/white rectangles in position round the square, and stitch by hand or machine, following the drawn lines. Press back.
3 Pin four 4.5 x 2.5 cm (1¾ x 1 in) black rectangles in place, and stitch. Press back.
4 Continue to sew alternating white/cream and black strips 2.5 cm (1 in) wide, and increasing in length, in position. Finish the square with four triangles of black fabric to cover the corners.
5 Sew two 13.5 x 2.5 cm (5¼ x 1 in) cream strips on two opposite edges of the square, and press back.

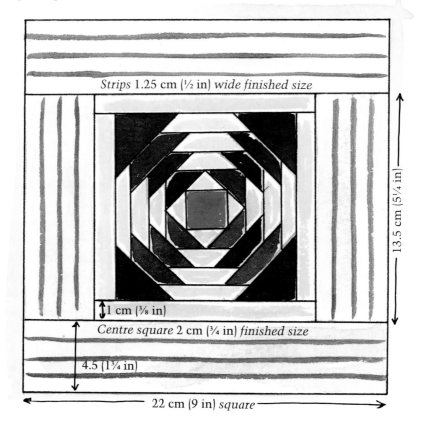

Strips 1.25 cm (½ in) wide finished size

13.5 cm (5¼ in)

1 cm (⅜ in)

Centre square 2 cm (¾ in) finished size

4.5 (1¾ in)

22 cm (9 in) square

6 Sew two 15 x 2.5 cm (6 x 1 in) cream strips on the opposite two sides and press back.

7 Sew two 15 x 7 cm (6 x 2¾ in) ticking rectangles on two edges of this square, press the rectangles back.

8 Sew two 24 x 7 cm (9½ x 2¾ in) ticking rectangles on the opposite two edges, press the rectangles back.

9 Make up the piping, and tack it in position. Tack and sew the backing fabric in place, with right sides facing. Leave a generous opening, 18 cm (7 in) long. Turn the right side out, fit cushion pad inside, and invisibly hand sew the opening closed.

This little cushion shows the versatility of a log cabin patchwork. The colour choice gives the design a timeless appeal; it would fit equally well into a traditional or modern setting.

Note: It is enjoyable to experiment with different log cabin effects. For example, a quilt design could have a large central block, surrounded by identical, but smaller blocks. Alternatively, a 'sampler' piece could be made by joining different block formations together.

Chapter 3
How to quilt

Quilting can be described as a textile sandwich, with the wadding (batting) providing the filling. A variety of methods are used to secure the layers together, and these can be simple and utilitarian, or complex and decorative. It is surprising how two identical quilt designs can be transformed by changing the type of fabrics used, the thickness of wadding, and the colour (or colours) of the quilting thread.

Quilting patterns have evolved throughout the world, and there is a universal quality to many of them; the same patterns are found in examples of quilting from all the continents, but they are executed in different materials and colours.

Hand quilting

This gives a 'softer' effect than machine quilting, and many traditional designs are associated with this method.

REQUIREMENTS
Fabric for top side of quilt
Fabric for reverse side of quilt
Polyester wadding (batting)
Quilting threads
Betweens needles
A marker pen or pencil
Tacking (basting) thread
A quilting frame (optional)
Basic sewing tools and equipment

Is a quilting frame necessary?
Large pieces of hand quilting will need to be worked in a frame or ring. (See **How to begin** page 14 for details on different types of quilting rings and frames.) Small pieces of quilting will not necessarily need a frame, but whether you choose to use a frame or not is a matter of personal choice.

Threads for quilting:
As with any thread used for hand sewing, never work with a long length of thread, as the thread can tangle and will easily be weakened by pulling through the fabric many times. Apart from tacking (basting) thread, never use a piece of thread longer than 60 cm (24 in) for these reasons.

It is common practice when quilting to run the thread over a piece of beeswax, for added strength.

(See **Getting started** page 22 for details on the different types of threads used for quilting.)

Wadded quilting:
In this form of quilting lines of hand or machine stitches are used to hold the fabric layers together.

(See **Getting started** page 21 for details on different types of wadding.)

Hand quilting stitches:

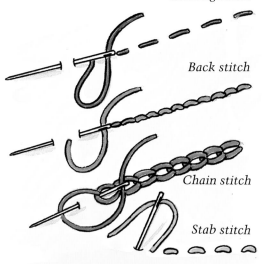

Running stitch

Back stitch

Chain stitch

Stab stitch

The stitches that are most frequently used for hand quilting are running stitch, stab stitch, back stitch and chain stitch. Back stitch and chain stitch both give a solid line, whereas running and stab stitches produce a broken line. Running stitch is the quickest to work, and gives a better effect than stab stitch, which looks similar on the front, but is almost impossible to work neatly on the reverse side of the quilt.

Note: When quilting or sewing by hand, always thread the end of the thread that comes off the spool. This is because thread has a twist, and so by sewing in the same direction as the twist, knotting and tangling will be avoided.

Always cut the thread, do not break it, as breaking the thread makes it more difficult to thread the needle.

This design is worked on red dyed cheesecloth and combines areas of hand quilting with contrast grids of machine quilting.

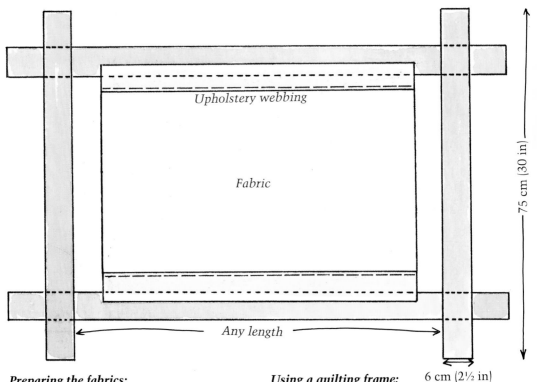

Upholstery webbing

Fabric

75 cm (30 in)

Any length

6 cm (2½ in)

Preparing the fabrics:

Mark the quilting design out on the top fabric, using a suitable marker.

If working *without* a frame, the top and backing fabrics and wadding need to be secured together, to prevent them moving while quilting. Do this by tacking the fabric layers together, using a tacking (basting) thread. Work the stitches so that they radiate out from the centre of the piece to the edge, and not just around the edge.

Using a quilting frame:

You can make a simple quilting frame from four pieces of wood batten, each 6 x 1.5 cm (2½ x 1½ in) thick. The back and front pieces (stretchers) can be as long as you wish, and the side stretchers should be about 75 cm (30 in) long. The four lengths are held together in the corners with small G clamps. Lengths of upholstery webbing are stapled or held with tacks to the front and back stretchers, and the quilting fabrics are tacked (basted) to the webbing.

To use a quilting frame: Begin by tacking (basting) the backing fabric, with wrong side facing upwards, to the webbing on the stretchers (the two long sides of the frame). Next, tack (baste) the wadding along one stretcher (this will be the one that you begin quilting from). Tack the top fabric to this stretcher, with the right side of the fabric facing upwards.

If you are quilting a large piece it will be necessary to roll the back stretcher over several times to make the frame a manageable size for working. To do this, roll the backing fabric around the stretcher, allowing the wadding and top fabric to hang loosely over the top of the back stretcher, or secure the fabrics out of the way with pins.

Now assemble the frame, attaching the two side battens. To secure the side edges of the fabrics, pin strips of tape or fabric through all layers and take them round the sides of the frame as shown. It is important not to pull the fabric too tightly, as this will make the fabrics difficult to quilt. The work should be held loosely. Some quilters use safety pins to secure the quilt in the frame, as it is easy to scratch yourself with dressmaker's pins, and of course, they may fall out. It is not necessary to do any further tacking (basting) when using a frame.

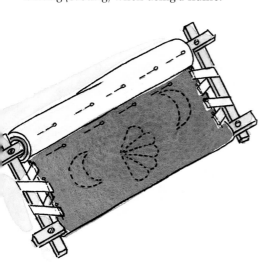

When the front edge of the piece has been quilted, undo the frame, unroll the back section, and roll the quilted section around the front stretcher. Re-assemble the frame, and continue the process until the whole piece has been quilted.

Working the stitches:

Start by following the marked out design. Use a needle appropriate to the thread being used; for a fine quilting thread use a betweens needle. You may find it helpful to try quilting stitches on spare fabric and wadding using different size needles.

Begin with a small knot on the end of the thread, and bring the needle up from the back of the work. Give the thread a tug, and the knot will go through the backing fabric and will be lost in the wadding. You will hear a 'ping' as this happens.

For running stitch, take as many evenly-sized stitches on to the needle as you can comfortably manage at a time, using a rocking movement to push the needle through the fabric. Make sure that the needle always passes right through the layers. You should feel the needle with the hand that remains under the work, so always work with one hand on top and one hand underneath.

At first it is best to make your stitches large, but even. This looks much better than stitches that vary in size. With practice you will probably find that your stitches become smaller. Always try to work the design by moving from one edge across the piece in an orderly way.

Changing thread:

When you reach the end of a piece of thread, make a small back stitch and bring the needle up through this stitch, splitting the thread as you do so. Then, take the needle into the layers, making sure that it does not go through to the back of the work. Bring the needle out about 2.5 cm (1 in) away, pull the thread tightly and cut it off. The thread end will be lost in the layers.

> **Note:** It is quite likely that you will prick your finger when quilting, in fact many quilters believe you should do so with every stitch made with the hand underneath, so you know that the stitches have passed through all the layers. This may result in drops of blood on the work. These can be removed in a time-honoured way by cutting a length of white thread, placing it in your mouth and chewing it until it becomes wet. Place it on the stain; it will act as a wick and absorb the blood.

Whole cloth quilt

This piece could be considered a sampler quilt, incorporating many different patterns. The ones chosen could easily be replaced with other patterns that you may have. A number of the patterns are derived from objects found around the home, such as biscuit cutters, shells, leaves, flowers and circles made by drawing round any suitable object. Look around and see what you can use for quilting patterns.

The patterns are arranged in an informal way in the centre of the quilt, within a formal border made of hearts.

Finished size 148 x 85 cm (58 x 33½ in).

REQUIREMENTS
*(All measurements are for fabrics 140 cm
    (54 in) wide, and are approximate.)*
1.70 m (2 yd) navy cotton
1.70 m (2 yd) yellow cotton
*1.70 m (2 yd) lightweight polyester
    wadding (batting)*
*Sewing/quilting threads in white, orange
    and cerise*
Sewing tools
A light coloured marker pen or pencil
A quilting frame or ring

1 Begin by cutting the top and backing fabrics and wadding to size, 150 x 87 cm (59 x 34½ in). Mark out the design on to the top fabric with the marker pen.
2 Place the backing fabric right side down, then place the wadding over this, followed by the top fabric, with right side facing upwards. If you are using a ring frame tack (baste) the top, backing fabric and wadding together. If you are using a large quilting frame put the fabrics and wadding in the frame as previously described.

Shells, whirls and fans and other quilting motifs appear at random around the central rosette. The heart border creates a formal frame.

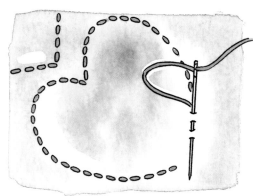

3 Follow the directions for working the quilting stitches, and work these with running stitch. Stitch different quilting patterns in different colours (you can vary these). Finish by including your name and date somewhere in the quilting.
4 When all the quilting is completed remove the work from the frame. Finish the edges by turning the top fabric under and the backing fabric under so that the sides are together. Sew a line of running stitches close to the edge.

Machine quilting

Machine quilting can be worked considerably faster than some forms of hand quilting. It appears quite different, and creates a strong linear effect, which can look much 'harder' than hand quilting. This is because the layers are very firmly attached together. It is easiest to quilt large pieces of work in sections, rather than in one large piece, as it can be quite awkward to attempt to machine stitch a large size quilt.

REQUIREMENTS
Fabrics and wadding as for hand quilting
A sewing machine with a 'walking' foot
Matching or contrasting sewing threads
Tacking (basting) thread
Basic sewing tools and equipment

Preparing to sew:

Before machine stitching, the fabric layers must be securely pinned or tacked (basted) together to prevent them 'creeping' under the machine. Secure the layers right across the surface, as for hand quilting.

Check the stitch tension and length. A 'walking' foot on the machine is a great help when machine quilting, as it stops the layers feeding through the machine at different rates. Without this aid distortion and puckering could occur.

As with hand quilting, work in an orderly method across the piece, and always try to stitch in the same direction.

White quilting stitches divide the eye-catching, blue and white triangles in this design.

A cot quilt

This project is a good introduction to machine quilting because it is an easy size to manage. Scraps of blue and white patterned fabrics are used, and these include plains, spots, striped shirtings and batik prints. Here the fabrics are arranged to shade diagonally from light to dark. You may, however, prefer another arrangement.

The finished size of this quilt will be 62 x 62 cm (24½ x 24½ in).

REQUIREMENTS
(All measurements are for fabrics 140 cm (54 in) wide, and are approximate)
Small amounts of blue and white patterned/plain cotton fabrics shaded from light to dark, sufficient for 50 triangles
50 cm (⅝ yd) blue and white patterned cotton
50 cm (⅝ yd) lightweight (2 oz) polyester wadding (batting)
2.50 m (3 yd) medium piping cord
25 cm (¼ yd) dark blue spotted cotton for piping
70 cm (⅞ yd) blue/white patterned cotton for the quilt backing
A marker pen or pencil
Matching sewing threads
Basic patchwork tools and equipment
A sewing machine
An iron
*(See **Making patchwork** page 43 for details on making pieced patchwork, and **How to make and finish a quilt** page 85 on making and attaching piping.)*

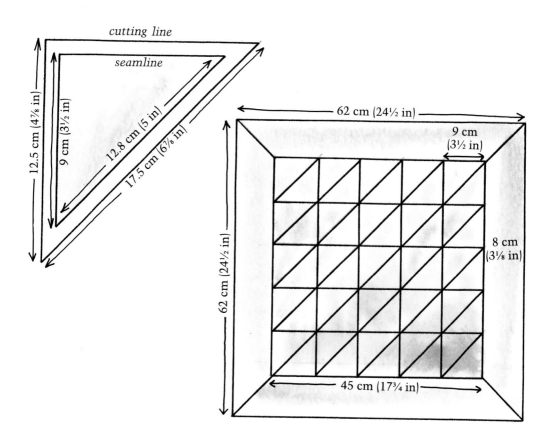

cutting line

seamline

12.5 cm (4⅞ in)

9 cm (3½ in)

12.8 cm (5 in)

17.5 cm (6⅞ in)

62 cm (24½ in)

9 cm (3½ in)

8 cm (3⅛ in)

62 cm (24½ in)

45 cm (17¾ in)

1 Cut the triangle patches from fabric following the measurements given in the cutting diagram. Carefully mark the seam lines on the reverse side of the patches.

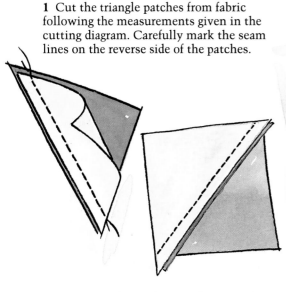

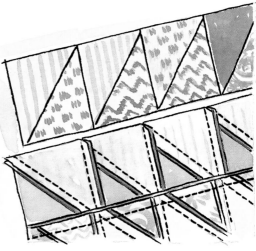

2 Sew pairs of triangles together to make squares following the directions for pieced patchwork. Sew these together by hand or machine. Press the seam allowance towards the darker colour fabric.

3 Join the squares together to make strips, then join these strips together, again pressing the seam allowance towards the darker fabric.
4 Cut the fabric for the border. Cut four pieces, each 10.5 x 64 cm (4½ x 25¼ in). Cut the ends of these pieces diagonally to make mitred corners.

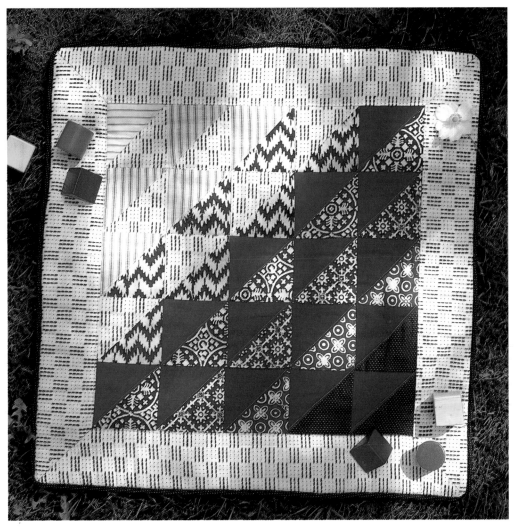

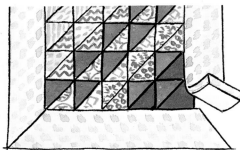

5 Sew these four border strips on to the patchwork square and press the seam allowance to one side. Sew the mitred corners and press these open.

6 Cut the wadding and backing fabric 64 x 64 cm (25¼ x 25¼ in).

7 To layer the fabrics, place the backing fabric right side downwards, and the wadding on top. Place the patchwork with right side facing upwards on the wadding. Pin and tack (baste) the layers together, stitching from the centre outwards.

8 Machine quilt in diagonal lines, carefully following the patchwork diagonals, then quilt around the inner edge of the border.

9 Make sufficient piping from the dark blue spotted cotton, (you will need about 2.50 m (3 yd) to bind the quilt). Pin and tack the piping around the edge, on the right side of the quilt, taking care to avoid the backing fabric. Machine stitch in place using a zipper foot. Turn and press the piping so that it faces outwards.

10 Pin and tack the backing fabric to the piping, and invisibly slip stitch in place.

Italian (corded) quilting

This decorative form of quilting, chosen for its beauty rather than warmth, employs thread or cord held between two layers of fabric. It is often worked with trapunto quilting and like this, it can be worked by hand or machine.

Examples of Italian quilting are to be found on eighteenth century garments and furnishings, where the craftsmanship displayed is exquisite. At this time it was worked on extremely fine white linen fabrics, with soft cotton thread for the quilting. The designs were delicate and naturalistic, and combined with drawn thread and pulled work.

REQUIREMENTS
Fabric for front of quilt
Backing fabric such as muslin (calico) or
  scrim
Wool or cord for quilting
A tapestry needle or bodkin
A marker pen
Matching colour threads for hand or
  machine stitching
Basic sewing tools and equipment

Fabrics for Italian quilting:
The best fabrics to use are fine cottons, linens, and silks or wools in light colours. The backing fabric needs to be loosely woven, such as muslin or linen scrim.

The work tends to shrink slightly in size when quilted, so allow for this in your initial measurements.

Thread for Italian quilting:
The thread that is most commonly used is a woollen thread produced especially for Italian quilting. This is a soft, cream untwisted thread. Obviously other threads can be used, and for a very delicate effect a thinner thread would need to be used.

If using Italian quilting wool, short lengths should be used (not more than 40 cm (16 in), to prevent it wearing.

Planning a design:
Mark out the design on the top fabric with a suitable marker. Parallel lines are generally used for this type of quilting. The space between these lines will vary, depending on the type of thread being used, but if using Italian quilting wool these should be placed at least 6 mm (¼ in) apart.

Preparing the fabrics:

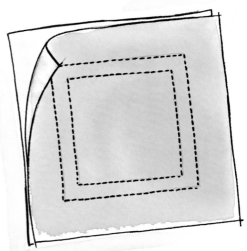

Pin and then tack (baste) the top fabric and the backing fabric together. Stitch round the pattern with a colour matching thread.

Threading the cord:

Working from the back and, pushing the fabric threads aside, use a blunt pointed needle to thread the wool into the channels made by the lines of stitching. When reaching corners or sharp curves in the design, take the needle back out through the backing fabric, then insert it again pointing it in the new direction. Leave a small tuft of wool at these points to prevent it from being pulled too tightly. (This would pucker and distort the surface.)

Shadow quilting

Coloured threads, fabrics or other materials are trapped between transparent or semi-transparent fabrics in shadow quilting. The top fabric is always transparent, or both fabrics can be. The muted colour of the filling shows through the top fabric.

This method is usually worked by machine, although it can be hand-stitched.

REQUIREMENTS
Transparent or semi-transparent top fabric
Fine fabric for backing
Coloured fabrics or ribbons
Matching or contrasting sewing threads
A marker pen or pencil
Double-sided fusible webbing (Bondaweb or double-sided Vilene) (optional)
Basic sewing tools and equipment

Fabrics and materials for shadow quilting:

Suitable fabrics for this type of quilting are fine cottons such as lawn, voile, organdie, muslin, or silks such as tulle, chiffon, georgette and organza. A fairly firm fabric should be used for the trapped fabric, such as closely woven cotton, felt or you may choose a firm woollen cloth.

A variety of trapped threads can be used from fine embroidery threads to thick wools and cords, but woollen threads are particularly suitable, because of their bulk, softness and excellent colour.

Always experiment with different effects, as even very bright or dark colours can be dramatically altered under the top fabric.

Other materials that can be trapped between the layers include: beads, sequins, seeds, rice, plastic, leather or paper.

Working shadow quilting:
Cut the fabric pieces for the top and backing layers. Prepare the materials for the middle, trapped layer. Pin these into place on the backing layer of fabric, or bond them in position with fusible webbing.

Place the top fabric layer over, and pin and tack it in place round the trapped shapes.

Stitching the shapes:
Machine or hand stitch around the outline of the trapped pieces, using a thread to blend or contrast with the top fabric.

Variations:
If trapping threads instead of fabrics, these can be held between the two layers, and then stitched in place as for fabric.

Try stitching lines or channels as for Italian quilting, and then insert threads or ribbons through these in the same way.

Thick, coloured yarns are threaded through fine, transparent fabric to create this vibrant design. A similar effect could be achieved with cords.

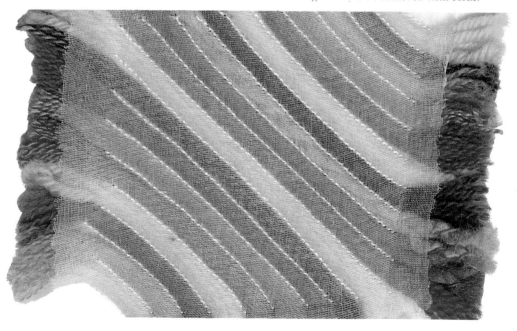

Trapunto quilting

In trapunto (stuffed) quilting, isolated areas or motifs have wadding inserted to create a relief pattern. The effect can be subtle, with small, gently rounded shapes, or more pronounced, depending on the design and the amount of wadding used. The method can be worked by hand or machine.

REQUIREMENTS
Fabric for front of quilt
Muslin (calico) or loosely woven fabric such as scrim for backing
Wadding
A marker pen or pencil
Small, sharp pointed scissors
A pointed tool, such as a thin knitting needle
Basic sewing tools and equipment

Working a design:

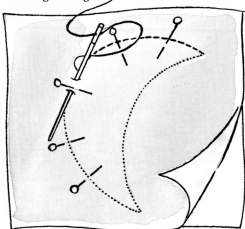

Transfer the design to the right side of the top fabric, and pin and tack (baste) this over the backing fabric. Stitch round the outline of the shape to be padded. You can use a running stitch or a back stitch for hand quilting, or use a machine straight stitch, perhaps in a contrasting colour, if this suits your style of design.

Cutting the backing fabric:

Cut a small slit in the backing fabric (taking care not to pierce the top fabric). With some loosely woven backing fabrics where very small amounts of wadding are to be inserted, it may be possible to push the threads of fabric aside to insert the wadding. The threads can then be gently stroked back into position.

Inserting the wadding:

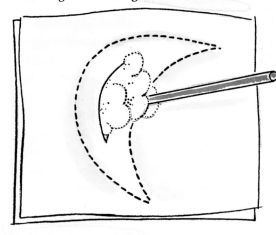

Gently push and ease the wadding through the opening using the pointed end of a knitting needle. The wadding should *lightly* pad the shape. Make sure that the wadding is evenly distributed and pushed right to the edges of the shape.

Stitching the opening:

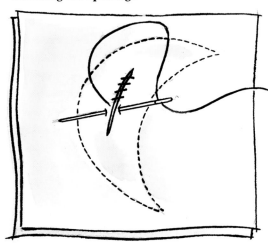

Sew the edges of the hole made in the backing fabric with small, overcast stitches. This will prevent the wadding from escaping, and will help to emphasise the padded surface.

> **Note:** *Trapunto quilting can be worked using contrast threads or transparent fabrics. Coloured filling such as dyed feathers can be used for decorative pieces.*

A pram quilt

Trapunto quilting is used in this quilt to provide a centre piece framed by log cabin strips. These are made from a variety of striped fabrics. The centre lily design could easily be replaced by a nursery image, such as an animal or toy.

The strips are made mostly from a delicately coloured Madras cotton with a pattern of stripes in varying colours and proportions. By using different sections of the same fabric in this way you can create the illusion of using several fabrics.

Finished size 56 x 47 cm (22 x 18½ in).

This delicate trapunto design has been worked with fabrics in pastel–nursery colours. The pink border could be replaced with blue, if desired.

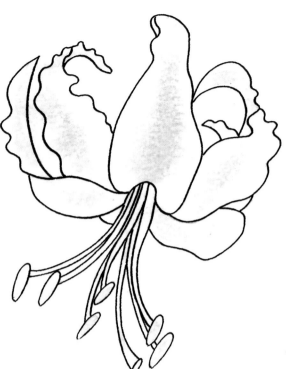

REQUIREMENTS
(All measurements are for fabrics 140 cm (54 in) wide, and are approximate.)
50 cm (⅝ yd) calico or lightweight cotton fabric (natural or white in colour) for patchwork backing
25 cm (⅓ yd) cream/ecru cotton lawn
Scraps of toning striped cotton fabrics
25 cm (⅓ yd) cream cotton
50 cm (⅝ yd) lightweight polyester wadding
Small amount polyester toy filling
50 cm (⅝ yd) striped cotton fabric (for quilt backing)
Basic sewing equipment
A fine marker pen or pencil
A sewing machine
An iron
*(See **Making patchwork** page 55 for details on making log cabin patchwork, and **How to make and finish a quilt** page 86 for details on binding a quilt.)*

You can enlarge the central lily motif on a photocopier. Follow the quilt plan to make up the log cabin surrounds and the border.

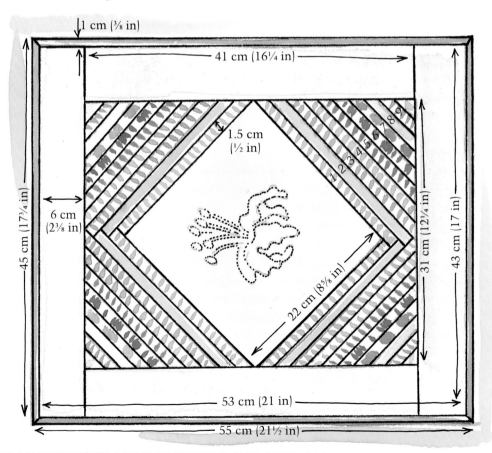

Making the patchwork:

1 Cut the calico backing fabric 33 x 43 cm (13 x 17 in). Mark the log cabin seam lines on the fabric with the marker pencil, following the design shown.

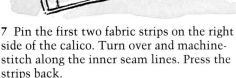

2 Cut the cream/ecru cotton lawn for the centre square 24 x 24 cm (9½ x 9½ in). Follow the design for the trapunto and draw the design on to the centre of the cotton lawn using the marker pen/pencil.

There are various ways to enlarge the central motif. You can enlarge the design on a photocopy machine, or you can trace it onto squared paper and then copy the outlines onto paper with larger size squares.

3 Tack (baste) this to the unmarked side of the calico.

4 Stitch round the lines either by hand or machine. If by hand, use a fine ecru cotton thread and a small running stitch; by machine use a darning foot to follow the design precisely.

5 Cut small slits in the calico backing fabric for each of the petal shapes to be padded. Push small amounts of the polyester filling through the slits. Avoid distorting the fabric by using too much filling.

6 Cut strips of fabric 3.5 cm (1⅜ in) wide for the log cabin. You require four strips of the same fabric for each 'round'. Nine groups of strips are required. Use the markings on the calico to estimate the length when cutting the strips.

7 Pin the first two fabric strips on the right side of the calico. Turn over and machine-stitch along the inner seam lines. Press the strips back.

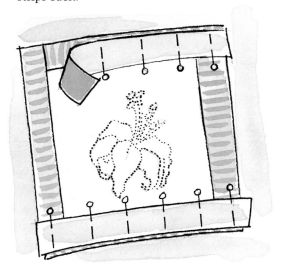

8 Pin the next two strips in position and machine-stitch them in place. Press these strips back.

> **Note:** *An easy way to draw a design on to a light coloured fabric is to place the fabric over the drawing, and to trace it. If the fabric and design are held up to a light source this is even easier. (You can tape both to a window, or place an unshaded table lamp under a glass topped table.)*

9 Continue with the other strips in the same way until they are all sewn in position. Trim away any excess fabrics from the edge of the calico.

The border and backing:

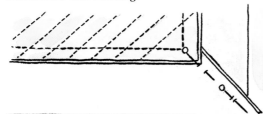

1 Cut four pieces of cream fabric for the border, two 58 x 10 cm (22⅞ x 4 in), and two 49 x 10 cm (19¼ x 4 in). Cut the ends of these strips at 45°. Stitch the four strips around the edge of the patchwork, then stitch the mitred corners. Press all the seams and the mitres, open flat.

2 Cut the backing fabric and a piece of wadding 56 x 47 cm (22 x 18½ in). Place the backing fabric right side down, and place the wadding on top of this, and the patchwork, with right side up, on top of the wadding. Pin and tack (baste) around the edge.

3 Cut the fabric for the binding from one of the striped fabrics. Cut strips 4 cm (1⅝ in) wide, and long enough to reach round the edge of the quilt. Pin the binding in position around the edge of the quilt and stitch close to the edge. Press the binding back. Turn the quilt over and the binding over the edge, then invisibly slip stitch the binding.

Tied quilting

The layers in wadded quilting can be tied together at points, rather than secured by lines of hand or machine stitching. This method does not hold the layers together as tightly as stitched quilting, but the advantages are that it is quick and easy to work, and is a good way of dealing with thick layers of fabric that would otherwise be difficult to sew.

REQUIREMENTS
Top fabric, wadding and backing fabric
Strong threads or other materials for ties
A needle with a suitably sized eye
Basic sewing tools and equipment

Suitable ties:

A strong thread that will stay securely knotted is the best to use. Woollen thread is particularly suitable because it will tend to felt holding the knot together. Other threads can provide interesting effects: linen, thicker cotton embroidery threads and silks, and very narrow ribbons. Of course, different coloured threads can also be used together in the needle.

Making ties:

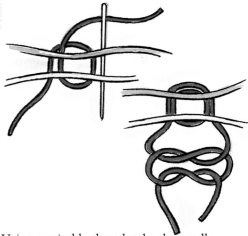

Using a suitable thread, take the needle vertically through the work from the back to the front, make a small stitch and then go through to the back of the piece again.

Bring the needle back up through the layers, beside the first stitch, then to the back of the piece beside the second stitch.

Pull the thread tightly and make a reef knot, then cut off the excess thread to make a tie on the back of the quilt.

To make a tie on the front of the quilt, start stitching from the front to the back.

Variations:

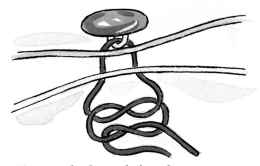

Ties can also be made from buttons, sequins or felt shapes and narrow ribbons.

Ties for quilting can be as simple or as decorative as you wish. Choose ties in a material and colour to suit the use of the quilt; make sure that they will clean or launder in the same way.

A wool throw with tied quilting

This is a quick and easy piece to make, based upon a bars design or 'strippy' quilts. It is composed of broad strips of contrasting colour fabrics. The colour combination could easily be adapted, but the colours selected here are rich and glowing.

Finished size 135 x 120 cm (53 x 47 in).

REQUIREMENTS
(All measurements are for fabric 140 cm (54 in) wide, and are approximate.)
40 cm (½ yd) red wool crêpe or challis
40 cm (½ yd) emerald green wool crêpe or challis
70 cm (¾ yd) lilac wool crêpe or challis
80 cm (¾ yd) burgundy wool crêpe or challis
145 x 125 cm (55 x 49 in) wadding (batting)
1.40 m (1½ yd) green cotton lining fabric
Matching sewing threads
1 skein red crewel wool embroidery thread
A sewing machine
Basic sewing tools and equipment
A suitable marker pen
An iron

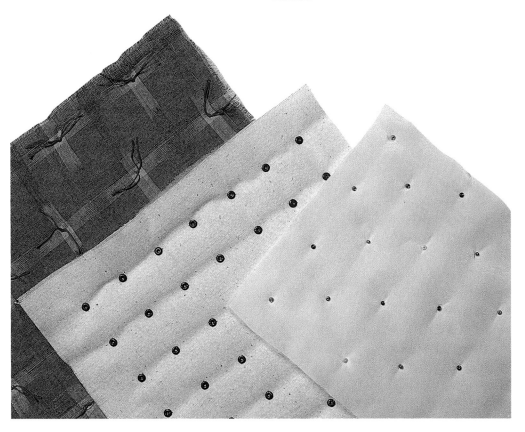

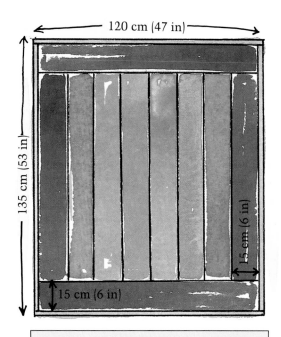

120 cm (47 in)

135 cm (53 in)

15 cm (6 in)

15 cm (6 in)

Follow the design layout to make this simple, tied throw. Because wool holds dye so well, the vibrant colours have a rich glow. For a different effect, other choices could be wool tweeds in muted heathery colours or, for a more delicate throw, fine soft wools in a mixture of creams, ecru and ivory would be luxurious.

Note: The throw could also be made using plain cotton fabrics, or striped fabrics, or a mix of patterns and plains. Ribbon could be substituted for the wool ties.

1 Cut 107 x 17 cm (42¼ x 6¾ in) strips of fabric as follows: two red, two green, two lilac, two burgundy. Cut two further burgundy strips 122 x 17 cm (48 x 6¾ in).
2 Machine stitch together the first eight strips in the arrangement shown, with right sides of fabric facing and taking 1.5 cm (⅝ in) seams. Press the seam allowances to the darker fabric.

4 Assemble the lining fabric, wadding and top of the throw together. Pin and tack (baste) together across the whole of the piece, and around the perimeter.

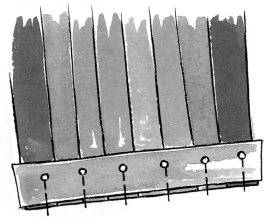

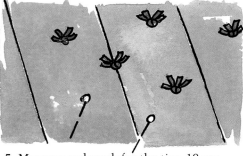

3 Join on the two larger strips of burgundy as shown and press the seam allowances towards the burgundy strips.

5 Measure and mark for the ties, 10 cm (4 in) apart. Tie the layers together with the red wool, arranging the ends evenly.

6 Cut four lilac strips for the binding, each 6 cm (2⅜ in) wide. Cut two about 125 cm (49 in) long, and two about 140 cm (55 in) long. Sew these in place along the edges of the right side of the throw, with right sides of fabric facing. Working on the top side of the quilt, sew the two shorter strips on to the short sides, followed by the longer strips on the other two sides. Press back.

7 Turn the binding over the edge of the throw and pin in position on the back. Tack (baste) in place, and invisibly hand stitch.

Chapter 4
How to complete a quilt

This chapter concentrates on ways to make up and finish a quilt. Allow plenty of time to do this well, as the quality will reflect on the whole piece. Some good advice is to try and work calmly in an ordered way, and never to continue to work if you are tired or unsure of what you are doing. Do not rush, as mistakes can easily be made if you hurry. Before making a quilt, plan the order in which you need to work. It is quite helpful to make a checklist:

1 Construct the top of the quilt
2 Join the borders
3 Prepare the wadding
4 Sew together fabric(s) to form the reverse side of the quilt
5 Attach the front, any wadding and reverse of the quilt by quilting, tying, or other method
6 Finish the edges of the quilt
7 Attach a sleeve or some means of hanging, if the piece is to be hung.

Reviewing your progress

When you are working, always be ready to change things if they do not look right. You may have planned a quilt carefully, but even so, when a piece starts to come together it can look quite different from how it was anticipated. Take a break now and again to see how the piece is progressing and, if you are unsure about any aspect of the design, stop for a while and return with a fresh eye.

If you can, leave the work pinned up overnight so that you can look at it early the next day. Frequently this fresh view will show clearly any aspects that are not working visually, even though these may not have been apparent before.

Borders

The right kind of border or edging will enhance the main section of the quilt, so choose these or other methods of finishing carefully, so that your choice is appropriate to the main piece. Make sure that the scale of the border is right for the overall scale of the quilt, and that the colour and type of fabric chosen is complementary.

Borders can frame a quilt, and provide a quiet space around a complex design. On a quilt designed for a bed, the border can be the part of the quilt that hangs over the sides, and so is not seen as clearly as the design on the top of the bed. In this case the border can be a simple design.

It is important to get the proportion between the centre of the quilt and the borders right, and this will vary from quilt to quilt. As a general rule, too small a border can look cramped, but a border that is too wide can overwhelm the centre of the quilt. Usually, you will be able to see when the sizes are suited.

Wadding (batting)

Wadding is available in quilt-sized pieces, but if you have not been able to obtain wadding in this form, smaller widths will have to be joined.

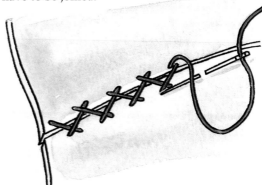

Joining wadding: Butt the pieces of wadding together. Do not overlap any joins as this would create a ridge which would show through the top fabric. Sew wadding together using a large herringbone stitch on one side, then turn the wadding over and stitch it on the reverse in the same way.

Backing fabrics

As these are an important part of the quilt, always choose good quality fabrics. Do not be tempted by inferior fabrics on the basis that they will not show, because they will. They will also appear unattractive and will not wear well.

Choosing backing fabrics: The colour and type of the backing fabric should relate to the fabrics used for the top of the quilt. Backing fabrics can provide an interesting contrast, or they may harmonize with the front of the quilt. Take care when using contrasting colour backing fabrics. For example, if the top of the quilt is very dark in tone, and lightweight wadding (batting) is used, a light colour for the backing would not be opaque enough to prevent the colour of the front showing through the lining.

Joining backing fabrics: If these need to be joined try to avoid having a seam running down the centre of the quilt. Keep the one width of fabric intact, but split the second width down the middle and join these two strips to each side of the intact piece.

Either trim the selvedges off the fabric or clip these with a small diagonal cut at regular intervals. Selvedges are frequently woven slightly tighter than the rest of the fabric, and when long lengths are joined the seam can pucker and pull.

Pipings

These are a good way of giving a crisp edge to a piece, and give cushions in particular a very finished look.

A piping cord is usually covered with a bias cut strip of fabric, which has more elasticity than fabric cut on the straight grain. Cord covered with bias cut fabric looks far better, and will fit round curves more easily than straight cut fabrics.

Piping cord is available in different sizes. Ensure you select a cord that is the right scale. If it is too large it can look clumsy.

Softer pipings can be made with bias cut strips of fabric folded double and used without piping cord.

Borders and pipings give a good finishing touch to a piece of work. They can be unobtrusive, in a colour to match the main piece, or they can be a definite design statement in their own right.

Making piping: Cut bias strips of fabric wide enough to cover the cord and leave a small seam allowance. Join bias strips as shown, to make a seam on the bias, and press the seams open flat.

> **Note:** To ensure a neat finish on piping, and to prevent possible distortion after cleaning, you can pre-shrink piping cord. To do this simply soak it for a while in boiling water and allow it to dry.

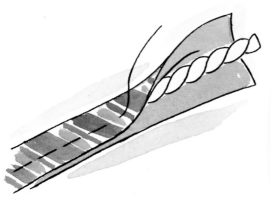

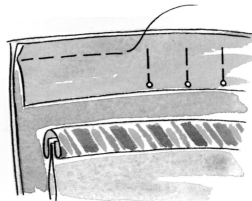

Pin and then tack (baste) the strip over the cord. Attach the piping to the main fabric as shown. To join piping ends, unstitch some of the fabric covering, and trim the cord to butt join, or unravel the cord threads and twist them together neatly. Overlap the fabrics, turning in the raw ends of the top

Press back the fabric and fold the strip round to the back of the quilt. Turn-in a small hem, then pin and tack (baste) the binding in position, and sew in place by hand.

Hanging quilts

You may make a piece that you intend to hang on a wall, or you may wish to exhibit your quilt in an exhibition. Both of these will require some method of hanging.

One of the methods described here will be the best for your purpose.

Fabric sleeve: The most common method for hanging a quilt is to sew a fabric 'sleeve' along the top edge of the piece. A wooden batten (or similar) is then inserted into the sleeve and this is attached to the wall.

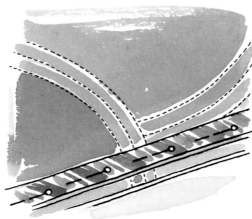

fabric, and tack (baste) to hold the piping securely before machine stitching. Machine stitch in place using a piping or zipper foot, stitching close to the cord.

Bindings

Bias cut lengths of fabric can be used to bind the edge of a quilt, as an alternative to borders. Because of their visual impact, striped fabrics make especially effective bindings. Bindings can also be made from fabrics cut on the straight grain.

Attaching bindings: For both bias cut and straight cut bindings, sew the strip first on to the front of the quilt (by hand or machine), with right sides of fabric facing.

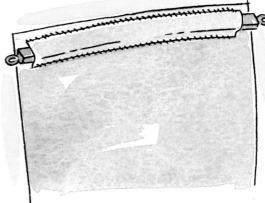

It is advisable to make the sleeve from double thickness fabric, so that the batten can be inserted between the two layers of fabric, as this will prevent any splinters in the wood from damaging the back of the quilt. Sew the sleeve in place with a slight tuck in the fabric to accommodate the thickness of the wood.

For large or very heavy quilts the sleeve can be made in two sections with a gap in the middle to provide an extra suspension point for the batten. This will prevent it bowing under the weight of the quilt.

A second sleeve with a narrower batten can be attached to the lower edge of the quilt if necessary, to help it to hang straight. The two ends of this sleeve can be closed with safety pins to prevent the batten sliding out or shifting.

Battens
Flat battens are preferable to lengths of dowelling or broom handles, as these tend to prevent the quilt hanging straight. Ensure that the wood you use is as straight and smooth as possible.

Using battens: Cut the wood slightly narrower than the width of the quilt, so that it will not protrude at each side or be visible from the front. Smooth the batten with sandpaper to ensure there are no splinters.

The batten can be screwed to the wall, or screw eyes can be inserted into the ends of the wood. These can then hang from nails or hooks in the wall.

Touch and close fastenings (Velcro)

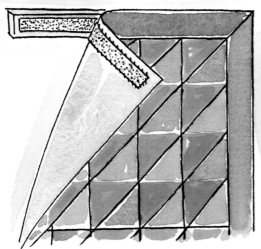

In this method, one side of a piece of Velcro is sewn to the top edge of the back of the quilt, and the other side is stapled to a wooden batten. The batten is attached to the wall and the back of the quilt is pressed against this, securing it in place. This method is most suitable for light or medium-weight quilts.

Loops and visible rod

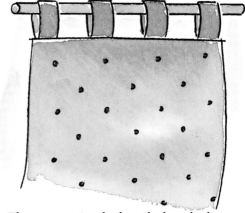

The two previously described methods are discreet and, if properly executed should not show; however you may wish the method of hanging to be visible if it is considered to be an integral part of the design.

If this is the case, sew loops to the top edge of the quilt and insert a rod or bar through these. These must be appropriate to the piece of work for this to be visually successful. The proportions of the loops should relate to the quilt, if they are too small they will not provide enough support and the quilt will droop and sag.

Rings stitched to the quilt back
For small wall pieces sew plastic or metal curtain rings at regular intervals on the back of the quilt, along the top edge. This method is only effective for very small pieces, it will not provide enough support for a large quilt.

> *Note:* You can hang or display quilts for a short time with large clothes pegs or with stationery bulldog clips. Attach these to the wall at regular intervals. Only use this method as a temporary measure.

Labelling
A label sewn to the back of your quilt with your name and the date your piece was made will provide interest for the future. Alternatively, this information could be included into the quilting design. If the work is to be sold it is advisable to attach this information to the piece, and to include washing or dry cleaning instructions.

A strip patchwork wall quilt

This wall quilt makes use of a wide variety of different types and colours of fabrics. These are selected to carefully shade through from light to dark, both in the strips and in the squares/triangles in each of the blocks. It is a good design for using many small strips and scraps of fabric left over from previous projects.

Finished quilt size 96 x 96 cm (38 x 38 in) square.

REQUIREMENTS
(All measurements are for fabric 140 cm (54 in) wide, and are approximate.)
Cutting note: *All strips for this quilt are cut 3 cm (1¼ in) wide, increasing in length from the shortest 9.5 cm (3¾ in) to the longest 23 cm (9 in)*
1.25 m (1½ yd) calico
Small amounts of a wide variety of different fabrics for the squares and triangles in: pinks, cerise, purples

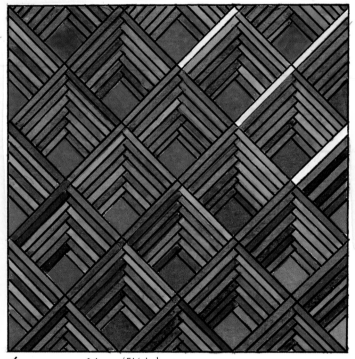

Copy the design layout to cut the strips for the quilt. It may be helpful to fill in the strips in your layout with coloured pencils to help you organize your fabric and cutting plan.

The colours chosen for this strip patchwork quilt give the design an intense, almost 3-dimensional quality, as the red and purple squares appear to be at the base of each green 'box'. The fabric strips shade from light to dark and show a definite log cabin influence.

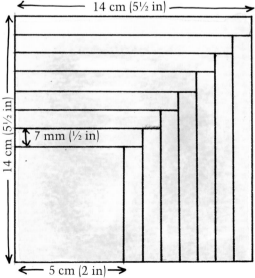

14 cm (5½ in)

14 cm (5½ in)

7 mm (½ in)

5 cm (2 in)

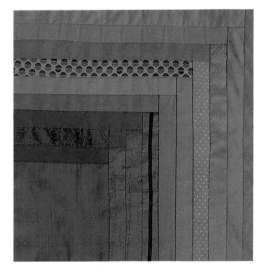

Small amounts of a wide variety of fabrics ranging through from light to dark for the strips in: greens, turquoise and blues

1.50 m (1¾ yd) jade green cotton for the binding, backing and sleeve

A marker pen or pencil, a rule and set square

Matching sewing threads

Sewing tools and equipment

A sewing machine

An iron

One skein lilac cotton perlé or similar embroidery thread

A wooden batten and two screw eyes

*(See **Making patchwork** page 55 for details on sewing log cabin, and **How to quilt** page 78 for details on tied quilting.)*

> **Note:** *It is a good idea to position yourself with your iron within reach of the sewing machine, as you will need to press each strip after it has been sewn in place. As pressing after each line of stitching is essential for a good finish, this saves time.*

Making the patchwork:

1 Cut the calico into twelve 23 x 23 cm (9 x 9 in) squares, and into twelve 31 x 23 cm (12¼ x 9 in) triangles.

2 Using a sharp marking pencil mark out the sewing lines on each of the squares and triangles, as accurately as possible.

3 Cut the fabrics for the pink/cerise/purple squares and triangles, and tack (baste) these in place on the side of the calico without the markings. Cutting sizes: squares 9.5 x 9.5 cm (3¾ x 3¾ in), triangles 13 x 9.5 cm (5⅛ x 3¾ in).

4 Cut the strips of fabric for one of the triangles which will form the top left-hand corner of the quilt. These should be the lightest colours from your palette of colours.

5 Arrange these in the order in which they are to be sewn in position (starting with the smallest). Sew these following the method for sewing strips for log cabin patchwork.

6 When one triangle is completed move on to the one which will go beside it, and follow the same method.

7 Proceed with all the other triangles and squares in the same way, gradually working across the quilt from the top left-hand corner to the bottom right-hand corner. The colours should become darker and richer across the quilt, ending with the darkest tone fabrics.

8 Machine stitch the triangles and squares together, first in strips, then sew the strips together. Press all the seams open.

Making the border and binding:

1 Cut a strip of green fabric 87.5 x 3 cm (34½ x 1¼ in) and sew it to the top edge of the quilt. Cut a strip of dark blue fabric to the same size and sew it to the bottom edge. Press the fabrics back towards the border. Cut two further strips, one green and the other dark blue, 90 x 3 cm (35½ x 1¼ in) and sew them to the other two sides. Press the fabrics back as before.

2 Cut two strips of jade green cotton 90 x 11 cm (35½ x 4⅜ in) and sew these to the top and bottom edges. Press the fabrics back. Cut two further strips of the same fabrics 98.5 x 11 cm (38¾ x 4⅜ in) and sew these to the other two sides. Press the fabrics back.

3 Cut a piece of jade green cotton 90 x 90 cm (35½ x 35½ in) square for the backing. Pin and tack (baste) this over the back of the quilt. Fold the edges of the binding over to the back and pin and tack (baste) them in place. Slipstitch the binding in position.

Tie quilting the finished piece:

Using the embroidery thread, tie the front and backing together at the corners of the squares. Each tie will disappear into the seam and will not be visible from the front.

Making the hanging sleeve:

1 Cut a strip of jade cotton 96 x 11 cm (37¾ x 4⅜ in), and hand or machine stitch a small hem along the two short sides. Press a seam allowance 1 cm (⅜ in) wide along the other two edges. Pin the sleeve along the top edge of the quilt, about 3 cm (1¼ in) from the edge. Hand stitch securely in place along the top and lower edges.

2 Insert the wooden batten with screw eyes at each end through the sleeve for hanging.

Caring for your quilt

When you have devoted much time and effort into making your quilt you should carefully consider the way it is to be kept.

It is important to protect all textiles from the damaging effects of dust, damp, insects and sunlight as much as is reasonably possible. It is also best to keep textiles in an even temperature. If a quilt is to be used on a bed or as a wall piece it should be kept out of direct sunlight. Sunlight both fades and weakens textile fibres. Even strong artificial lighting such as spotlights can be damaging.

Dust can be quite acidic, eventually rotting textile fibres, and obviously the presence of dirt dulls their appearance.

Storage

The best way to store a quilt is flat on a bed, with no folds and no weight placed on top of it, and with a clean cotton sheet as a covering. However, this does take up considerable space, particularly if you have a number of quilts to store. The alternatives are folding or rolling round a tube.

Unwrap stored quilts periodically to inspect their condition, and to re-fold them in a different way to prevent any permanent damage along the folds. Mothballs will help prevent attack from moths and other destructive insects.

Whichever way you store your quilt, remember, *NEVER* store textiles in plastic bags: plastic does not 'breathe' and fabrics can become mouldy.

Folding: The simplest way to store a quilt is to fold it with the right side out, preferably with sausage-shaped rolls of acid-free tissue paper placed along the folds. This helps to prevent creasing. Wrap the quilt in more acid-free tissue paper or in a clean cotton sheet, and place it in a box, drawer or chest lined with more acid-free tissue.

Rolling: Different tubes can be used to roll quilts around: cardboard tubes used for fabric or carpets, plastic drainpipes or, for smaller pieces, use water-pipe insulating covers which are sturdy and lightweight.

The tube should be slightly longer than the width of the quilt, and should be first covered with a layer of polyester wadding or acid-free tissue paper. Roll the quilt loosely round the tube with the right side to the outside. Enclose it in a piece of clean fabric large enough to completely enclose the quilt, and loosely tie it at intervals with cotton tape.

Ideally, rolls should be hung to prevent pressure on any one part of the quilt, but this is rarely possible in the domestic situation. Laying the roll flat is preferable to storing it vertically, because the quilt could easily slip down the tube and become crumpled at the base.

Cleaning your quilt

Quilts should be kept free of dust and dirt without laundering them too frequently. Removal of dust with a feather duster or vacuum cleaner should be done regularly.

Vacuum cleaning: Do this gently, using an upholstery attachment on low suction. Either keep the attachment just above the surface of the quilt or cover the end with a piece of fine fabric (net or muslin would be suitable). This prevents the fabric or any loose threads being sucked into the nozzle. Both the front and the back of the quilt should be vacuumed.

Dry cleaning: This should be undertaken by a specialist cleaner, or by a textile conservationist. Do not use a commercial cleaner, as the solvents used could do considerable damage. Consult a museum or quilters' guild for specialist advice.

Washing: Ideally this should be done by hand, but some quiltmakers wash their

quilts by machine with excellent results!

Some quilts should not be washed, so consider carefully before deciding to wash a quilt. Old, damaged or fragile quilts could be further damaged by washing.

The dyes in fabrics that are not colourfast could run and ruin a quilt. Always check for colour fastness before washing a quilt by placing a piece of damp cotton wool on an unobtrusive part of the quilt. If the dye is not fast some of the colour will transfer to the cotton wool.

The best way to wash a quilt is in the bath. Use lukewarm water and a delicate agent such as soap flakes. Many modern detergents are far too harsh to use on a delicate quilt. Use plenty of water and lower the quilt gently into the bath. Leave it to soak for about an hour, do not rub or scrub the quilt, but very gently agitate it to loosen the dirt in the fibres. Let the water drain out. Rinse the quilt in plenty of lukewarm water, until the water runs clear. You can also use a shower attachment with gentle water pressure for rinsing.

Avoid lifting or moving the quilt as much as possible. Leave it to drain for some time (this could be several hours in the case of a large quilt). Place it in a large plastic bag or sheet and take it to dry outside. It may be best to get someone to assist you with this. (If the quilt is very sturdy, it may be possible to spin it in a washing machine on the spin dry programme for a short time, but do not attempt this if the quilt is delicate.)

Dry the quilt laid flat on a clean sheet, out of strong sunlight. It is not advisable to use a washing line, as the quilt can be distorted or damaged by the weight of the wet quilt hanging from a single point.

Ensure that the quilt is completely dry before storage.

Cleaning with bread: this is a good way of removing surface dirt and dust from a quilt without washing. Use the bread as you would a pencil eraser.

Use fresh white bread and break off small pieces; use these to gently rub the surface of the quilt. (A large quilt may take a large loaf of bread to clean it thoroughly.) The bread will soon form small grey rolls as it absorbs the surface grime. These can be gently brushed off by hand. When the entire quilt has been cleaned it can then be vacuumed following the instructions given previously.

Further reading

Allen, Rosemary E. *North Country Quilts and Coverlets from Beamish Museum*. Beamish, County Durham, 1987.

Barker, V. & Bird, T. *The Fine Art of Quilting*. London, Studio Vista, 1990.

Bishop, Robert and Safanda, Elizabeth. *A Gallery of Amish Quilts*. New York, Dutton, 1976.

Campbell-Harding, Valerie. *Strip Patchwork*. London, Batsford, 1983.

Colby, Averil. *Patchwork*. London, Batsford, 1983.

Colby, Averil. *Quilting*. London, Batsford, 1983.

Fox, Sandi. *Wrapped in Glory: Figurative Quilts and Bedcovers 1700–1900*. New York & London, Thames and Hudson, 1990.

Hake, Elizabeth. *English Quilting, Old and New*. London, Batsford, first published 1937, reprinted 1988.

Holstein, Jonathan. *The Pieced Quilt*. New York Graphic Society, 1973.

James, Michael. *The Quiltmaker's Handbook*. Prentice Hall, 1978.

Liddell, Jill. *The Changing Seasons: Quilt Patterns from Japan*. Dutton & Penguin, 1992.

Short, Eirian. *Quilting: Technique, Design and Application*. London, Batsford, 1979.

Walker, Michele. *Quiltmaking, in Patchwork and Appliqué*. London, Ebury Press, 1985.

Useful addresses

Great Britain
Crafts Council
44a Pentonville Rd
London N1 9BY
England

The Quilters' Guild
OP66
Dean Clough
Halifax
West Yorkshire HX3 5AX
England

National Patchwork Association
P.O. Box 300
Hethersett
Norwich
Norfolk NR9 3DB
England

Suppliers
Beckfoot Mill
Clock Mill
Denholme
Bradford
West Yorkshire BD13 4DN
England
(Mail order service. Polyester wadding in different weights and widths.)

Quilt Basics
2 Meades Lane
Chesham
Bucks. HP5 1ND
England
(Mail order service. Equipment for patchwork and quilting.)

Strawberry Fayre
Chagford
Devon TQ13 8EN
England
(Mail order service. Cotton fabrics and quilting supplies.)

Australia
The Quilters' Guild Inc. of Australia
P.O. Box 654
Neutral Bay Junction
New South Wales 2809
Australia

Quilts Down Under (magazine)
P.O. Box 629
Beeleigh
Queensland 4207
Australia

New Zealand
Crafts Council of New Zealand
22 The Terrace
Wellington
New Zealand

New Zealand Quilter
(magazine)
P.O. Box 9202
Wellington
New Zealand

Canada
Canadian Quilters' Association
P.O. Box/C.P. 22010
Heron Gate Postal Outlet
Ottawa
Ontario KIV 0C2
Canada

United States of America
American Quilters' Society
P.O. Box 3290
Paducah
KY 42002-3290
USA

Quilter's Newsletter (magazine)
Box 394
Wheatridge
Colorado 80034-0394
USA

DMC Corporation
107 Trumball Street
Elizabeth
New Jersey 07206
USA
(Embroidery threads suitable for different types of quilting.)

Index